MOBILE
MARKETING

**Fundamentals
and
Strategy**

KAAN VARNALI — AYSEGUL TOKER — CENGIZ YILMAZ

NEW YORK   CHICAGO   SAN FRANCISCO
LISBON   LONDON   MADRID   MEXICO CITY   MILAN
NEW DELHI   SAN JUAN   SEOUL   SINGAPORE
SYDNEY   TORONTO

The McGraw·Hill Companies

1 2 3 4 5 6 7 8 9 0   DOC/DOC   1 5 4 3 2 1 0

ISBN: 978-0-07-174302-0
MHID: 0-07-174302-2

This publication is designed to provide accurate and authoritative information in regard to the subject matter covered. It is sold with the understanding that neither the authors nor the publisher is engaged in rendering legal, accounting, securities trading, or other professional services. If legal advice or other expert assistance is required, the services of a competent professional person should be sought.

—*From a Declaration of Principles Jointly Adopted by a Committee of the American Bar Association and a Committee of Publishers and Associations*

Library of Congress Cataloging-in-Publication Data
Varnali, Kaan.
    Mobile marketing / by Kaan Varnali, Aysegul Toker, Cengiz Yilmaz. — 1st ed.
    p. cm.
    Includes bibliographical references and index.
    ISBN 978-0-07-174302-0 (alk. paper)
    1. Telemarketing. I. Toker, Aysegul. II. Yilmaz, Cengiz. III. Title.
    HF5415.1265.V367 2010
    658.8'72—dc22

                                                                        2010032042

McGraw-Hill books are available at special quantity discounts to use as premiums and sales promotions or for use in corporate training programs. To contact a representative, please e-mail us at bulksales@mcgraw-hill.com.

This book is printed on acid-free paper.

Contents

4   The Future of Mobile Marketing

Foreword

In the beginning of the new millennium, sending basic text messages to customers was considered by many companies to be highly innovative. Today, however, mobile technology is vastly more robust and people are far more confident in using it. So much so that in many societies people have become "mobile-dependent"—and we are coming toward the end of the first generation of mobile users. The latest advances in mobile technology enable the creation of mobile services that are engaging, interactive, and entertaining. As mobile handsets proliferate in terms of usability and graphic interface, the mobile medium is on the verge of becoming the optimal platform available for direct customer contact. Today, the mobile medium presents unprecedented opportunities to marketers to deliver highly personalized messages to their target customers through a multitude of innovative applications such as SMS, MMS, IVR, the mobile Internet, RBT, sponsored info packages, mobile coupons, mobile games, mobile tickets, mobile tags, mobile payments systems, and location-based services.

The impact of mobile on the traditional time cycles of marketing, segmentation, and targeting, as well as the creation of uniquely personalized marketing, have created an entirely new competitive environment in almost every industry. For example, the response rates of Turkcell's mobile advertising campaigns vary from between 5 percent and 25 percent. The average response rate is 9.2 percent, far higher than traditional advertising methods and a fact that clearly illustrates the need to integrate mobile within a company's existing communication channels. The challenge is that mobile marketing offers unique value propositions to both consumers and the advertisers, if, and only if, its true essence is properly understood by everyone in the mobile value chain. That's why Turkcell is willing to take an active role in educating the market about the unique characteristics of the mobile medium in order to facilitate the adoption of mobile marketing practices. As well as being directly involved in the design and implementation of mobile marketing campaigns, we actively participate in international and local marketing conferences, organize workshops and seminars with global brands, and pursue collaborative opportunities with a number of universities throughout the world. In line with this approach, we have shared our award-winning market knowledge and experience with the authors of this book and have seen the creation of a milestone reference book for anyone with an interest in the phenomenon that is mobile marketing.

This book provides an overall, up-to-date picture of the mobile marketing landscape. I believe its value lies both in its ability to clearly present current, accumulated academic thinking about the mobile medium and mobile consumer behavior and in the way this academic perspective is illustrated with facts and figures from Turkcell's rich portfolio of mobile marketing case studies. It includes an up-to-date list of mobile services and applications, compares their features and value propositions with those of the traditional media, and elaborates on the unique challenges and benefits of mobile. The strategic model presented provides a basis for establishing best practices across the mobile value chain. I strongly believe that this book is a must-read for everyone involved in the mobile ecosystem and that it also acts as a practical and easy-to-read reference book for academics, students of marketing, and anyone looking to start in the business of mobile marketing. I hope you find it an interesting and enjoyable read.

Süreyya Ciliv
CEO Turkcell

Acknowledgments

This book has benefited greatly from a number of recent examples of Turkcell's cutting-edge mobile marketing campaigns. We believe that those examples have improved the book's relevance to practical mobile marketing issues substantially. We would therefore like to extend our sincere gratitude to the many members of the Turkcell family who wholeheartedly supported us throughout the entire research and writing process.

Firstly, we would like to thank Esra Ekin Ramazanoglu from Turkcell Academy for her efforts in bringing together academia and the mobile industry to share and disseminate knowledge. Without her energy and dedication, none of this would have been possible. Starting with Melis Turkmen, Banu Kargın, and Aslı Kaplan, we would also like to thank all the members of Turkcell's mobile marketing team for meeting with us many times, for reading and commenting on our drafts, and for all the information they have generously shared. It was a huge pleasure to work with you guys every step of the way, and we really appreciate your help and kindness. Special thanks to all those who stepped in and helped us when we needed specific assistance, particularly during the final edit of the book.

Special thanks go to Malcolm Gladwell for providing us with our first testimonial quote.

And, finally, many thanks to our families, friends, and colleagues who inspired and encouraged us throughout. It is impossible to exaggerate your role in the creation of this book.

1

Defining Mobile Marketing

The Mobile Revolution

The term *technology* is defined as scientific knowledge applied to useful purposes (Capon and Glazer, 1987). Technology has been the primary driver of productivity and market growth since the Industrial Revolution. Today, technological progress is occurring at an ever-increasing pace. New technologies do not compete only with old ones at a primary level that is usually the attribute perceived to have the greatest importance by customers, but they also introduce novel dimensions that offer a new basis of competition or way of doing business. Old technologies may be completely defenseless against these new changes (Sood and Tellis, 2005).

When a new technology represents such a discontinuity in the marketplace, companies have no choice but to adopt that technology if they want to remain competitive. The proliferation of the mobile medium and its use for customer interaction represents such a change, which has been popularized by the term "mobile revolution." In the rest of this book, we elaborate on the unique challenges and benefits presented by the mobile revolution, analyze the mobile medium in terms of its consumer-centric value propositions, describe the set of mobile applications and the underlying technologies that enable delivery of these value propositions, and discuss the tremendous impact of mobile technology on the universe of marketing.

Mobile phones were originally introduced as a new form of interpersonal communication, allowing people continuous communication while they are on the move. Recent developments in the mobile technologies, both in the capabilities of hand-held devices and in the underlying infrastructure, converted the mobile channel into a complex business space in which business entities launch various kinds of marketing campaigns utilizing text messaging, multimedia services, and mobile Internet. Now mobile users do not only communicate with each other through the mobile medium, but they also engage in various types of services provided by business entities. For example, they shop and entertain themselves.

Moreover, the penetration rate of mobile handhelds has well passed that of landline phones, PC-based Internet devices, and any other technological innovations. According to Juniper Research (2008a) penetration rate of mobile handsets exceeded 100 percent in western Europe in 2006, and in eastern Europe the mark was reached in 2007. The mark has also been reached in several Middle Eastern and Asian-Pacific countries as well. The penetration rate in the Americas is also rising steadily and is currently above 80 percent.

According to the Turkish Statistical Institute, the household ownership rate of mobile phones in Turkey exceeded 87 percent by the end of 2009, which is much higher than that of PCs and laptops, which are 27 and 8.5 percent, respectively (see Figure 1.1). Figure 1.2 shows the increasing disparity between the number of mobile subscribers and landline subscribers in Turkey. The popularization of mobile technology, improvements in handsets, and the growth in its business potential, gave rise to the phenomena called "mobile marketing."

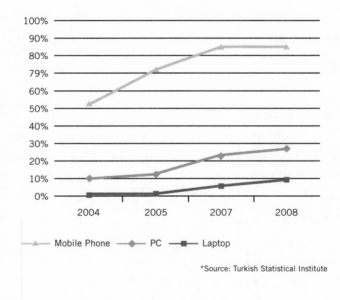

FIGURE 1.1 HOUSEHOLD DEVICE OWNERSHIP RATES IN TURKEY

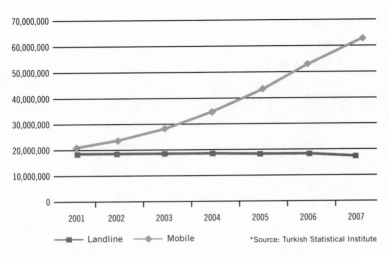

FIGURE 1.2 MOBILE VERSUS LANDLINE SUBSCRIBERS IN TURKEY

What Is Mobile Marketing?

Mobile marketing covers a large set of applications which basically revolutionized the way modern companies conduct their business. Unlike any other existing media, mobile marketing enables distribution of interactive and personalized information to the consumer at the most appropriate time and place and in the right context (Mort and Drennan, 2002), and it provides an unprecedented opportunity to establish a direct link with the consumer. The space-time paradigm on which traditional marketing is based implodes into the "virtual now" of the network age (Berthon, Pitt, and Watson, 2000) and introduction of mobile technology into the business space is the ultimate catalyst of this transition.

Thanks to advancements in mobile technologies and utilization of them in customer service, many daily activities became spatially and temporally flexible. Now it is possible for one to conduct financial transactions or book a flight while waiting in line at the supermarket. Mobile services allow subscribers not only to engage in their routine activities conveniently while they are on the move, but they provide updates about various kinds of news anytime, anywhere. Traffic, weather, sports, news, stock exchange updates, and promotional messages are among many kinds of notifications that subscribers can opt into receive. In addition, the music, video, and gaming capabilities of mobile devices entertain mobile users during the slow points of the day. The inherent characteristics of mobile devices such as "exceptionally personal," "always with the user," "always connected," and "always on," when combined with the aforementioned technological capabilities, make mobile marketing the ultimate tool for one-to-one marketing and an extremely powerful tool for customer relationship management (CRM).

Mobile marketing is the creation, communication, and delivery of customer value through the wireless, mobile medium. It has a significant impact on the entire value creation chain of companies both by enhancing existing and prospective customer communication, service, and support through cheap, measurable, interactive, highly personalized and well targeted information delivery and by improving internal communications and operations.

Use of Mobile Technologies within the Customer-Company Interface

The penetration rate of mobile devices is so high, even higher than wired PC-based Internet and landline telephony, that the owners of mobile handheld devices represent a large group of potential customers. These devices can be considered as smart gadgets of technology in pockets of individual customers who are connected to the databases of enterprises. This one-to-one–based connection provides an unprecedented opportunity for ultimate customer relationship management. The mobile medium allows creation, communication, and delivery of customer value through consumer-centric mobile services and interactive mobile applications. Mobile services and applications appeal to consumers by providing ubiquitous personalized service throughout their daily activities. Thanks to these mobile services, mobility no longer limits people's productivity or businesses' ability to reach their existing and potential customers.

Short Message Service

Text messaging is an evolutionary form of direct marketing. It was introduced in 1992 as a novel form of passive advertising delivered to mobile phones of potential customers. Today, uses of text messaging in mobile marketing campaigns vary from simple passive brand advertisements, to interactive response-seeking messages and personalized special offers. Short message service (SMS) allows a 160-character text-only format. Thus mobile marketers are presented a huge challenge to create highly personalized, attention grabbing, and interesting messages. SMS messages have proven to be most effective when they are permission-based, include an incentive, are highly personalized, and are delivered at the right time and place. The most widely used mobile campaign incentive types are free airtime, branded mobile content (music, video, games, wallpapers, ringtones, etc.), participation in competitions, and votes. The uniqueness of SMS marketing lies in its potential to target consumers in a specific context.

Mobile marketing campaigns use SMS messages in interactive integration with television, PC-based wired Internet, and printed advertising. SMS is a beneficial interactive marketing tool because the use of SMS is easy, cheap, and instant from the customers' perspective.

Another important advantage of SMS advertising over television and print media advertising is that it can be conveniently stored in the memory of the handheld device and referred to when needed in the future. A stored SMS message may act as a reminder of the advertisement each time a user takes a look at his or her inbox.

SMS marketing can have a significant branding effect and influence on purchase intentions. Rettie, Grandcolas, and Deakins (2005) evaluated the effectiveness of 26 different SMS advertising campaigns. The average response rate for SMS advertising was found to be 31 percent, which is significantly higher than that of permission-based direct mail (1–8 percent). Although a strong branding effect was found, the authors identified a strong correlation between call to action and brand recall. It is highly probable that taking the action might be reinforcing brand recall. Therefore, an SMS used just to advertise a brand may not be effective unless it calls for action. (See Exhibits 1.1 through 1.3.) The study also found that perceived relevance of the SMS content significantly influences purchase intention, which suggests the importance of creativity in developing 160-character text-based messages, personalization of the content, and targeting.

EXHIBIT 1.1   DORITOS' SMS-BASED MOBILE VOTING
CAMPAIGN IN 2004

In line with findings of academic research, most mobile campaigns
are designed to include an incentive-based call-to-action component to increase customer involvement. Doritos, for instance,
asked its customers to suggest a name for its new product via SMS
in 2004. The mobile user whose suggestion was chosen to be the
name of the product was rewarded with a Smart Roadster.

EXHIBIT 1.2 DORITOS' SMS-BASED MOBILE VOTING
CAMPAIGN IN 2005

In 2005, Doritos asked young consumers the following question:
"Money or love?" The campaign was very successful in drawing
public attention and generating responses, such that the question
became the central issue of debate in written and visual media
during the time of the campaign. Each week, five couples among
the ones who chose "love" were rewarded with a vacation to Ibiza,
and five users among the ones who chose "money" were rewarded
with a debit card loaded with 1,000TL. The campaign was so successful that it increased sales revenue of Doritos by 30 percent
permanently by increasing brand awareness among young people.
Doritos was happy with the success of its mobile campaigns and
had allocated approximately 20 percent of its marketing budget to
the mobile medium in 2008.

EXHIBIT 1.3 AKBANK'S SMS-BASED MOBILE CREDIT APPLICATION CAMPAIGN

Akbank, a Turkish bank, launched an innovative mobile campaign in which it accepted personal credit applications via SMS. All the users had to do was text their national identity number to the bank and wait for the bank's response. The bank promised to respond to all SMS credit applications within 20 minutes without any further questions. Akbank first initiated the campaign with its own client database, and then went nationwide using the permission-based subscriber database of Turkcell. The campaign was a great success. The return rate was 20 percent, which was an excellent number when compared to the prior experience of the bank with traditional mail and e-mail with a return rate of only 1 to 2 percent. The company not only facilitated credit demand from the existing customers, but it also introduced new valuable customers to the bank as well.

Another type of SMS-based advertising provides subscribers with sponsored information updates such as weather/traffic reports, financial updates, and notifications about sports events. Companies use such services to establish an association with their brands and specific events or situations (see Exhibit 1.4).

Another type of mobile marketing campaign is to call people to action by offering premium SMS to people to participate in radio and TV contests such as radio playlist surveys, favorite hit charts, TV shows, competitions, and political surveys. The media viewer is instructed to send a text message consisting

EXHIBIT 1.4 SPONSORED SMS NOTIFICATIONS

Lipton has sponsored text-based weather updates in order to create a mental association with hot weather and refreshing Lipton Ice Tea.

of a short code, and the system responds to the user by confirming participation and charges a premium to the phone bill. TV shows such as American Idol have generated phenomenal response rates and revenues world-wide via premium SMS votes.

SUMMARY: USES OF SMS

- Passive text message advertising
- Timely teasers (contextually congruent messages)
- Branded slogans at the end of sponsored messages
- Voting and polls
- Competitions
- Discount coupons/special offers
- Credit applications
- *CRM-based messages.* Timely information about weather, traffic, sports events, financial markets, news, and so on
- *Micropayments.* Premium-rate SMS can be used as a means to pay for mobile content

---

Enhanced Messaging Service

Enhanced messaging service (EMS) is an extension of SMS that was introduced in the late 1990s to add some functionality to plain-text SMS messages. EMS technology makes it possible for short text messages to include special text formatting and predefined simple graphics. The most important inhibitor of the widespread adoption of EMS messaging was the fact that not all devices were supporting the technology. Another problem was that there were very few additional benefits that only a few operators introduced. EMS messages that are sent to devices that do not support it are displayed as SMS messages, which may be unreadable because of the presence of additional data that cannot be interpreted by the device.

As the interoperability limitations started to disappear and most of the handheld devices started to support EMS technology, EMS messages became the underlying technology for an innovative mobile marketing application that is mobile coupons. EMS allows delivery of digital coupons to the mobile handheld devices that can be identified by bar code readers at shops and markets. Mobile coupons do not only represent a convenient way of payment for mobile users, but they also allow marketers to provide consumers with customized discount tickets (see Exhibit 1.5). Mobile coupons that are stored in the phone have higher redemption rates than paper or e-coupons because they

EXHIBIT 1.5. AN EXAMPLE OF A MOBILE COUPON

are not forgotten or left at home. Mobile coupons can drastically reduce delivery and redemption costs. When delivered at the right time and place, mobile coupons are effective promotion vehicles that can trigger impulse buys.

Mobile coupons are expected to boost usage of coupons as a whole. People who are reluctant to carry a bunch of coupons will be more apt to use them with the clean, fast coupon retrieval process. For those who have been embarrassed to present coupons at restaurants, this new technology will allow for a more delicate transaction to take place. Users of a mobile coupon may actually look rather tech-savvy using their digital coupon instead of looking like a person who is either overly frugal or poor, and looking for a discount.

Apart from being used in mobile coupons, mobile bar codes are also used in mobile ticketing (see Exhibit 1.6 for an example of an m-ticket for an event targeting young people). Mobile tickets are particularly useful in the transportation ticketing sector, where commercial trials had been successfully deployed in the Far East, western Europe, and North America. Benefits for ticket issuers include reduced costs, better security to help the fight against fraud, and an improved environmental record by reducing paper. For instance, a Juniper Research (2008b) report argued that the airline industry could achieve savings of $500 million per year by migrating to mobile boarding passes. The same report forecasted a total of nearly $87 billion worth of mobile ticketing transactions by 2011.

Apart from convenience issues, another significant advantage of mobile bar codes over traditional paper-based coupons or tickets is the "green factor." Digital coupons are environmentally friendly because their production requires no paper or ink, and their disposal does not result in pollution.

EXHIBIT 1.6.   AN EXAMPLE OF A MOBILE TICKET

Multimedia Messaging Service

Multimedia messaging service (MMS) messages are very much
like SMS messages, but they can also incorporate pictures, audio,
and video clips. MMS has not proved to be as successful as was
predicted when it was introduced as an extension of SMS. The
main reasons for that are slow download rates and the high price
of the wireless application protocol (WAP) service that the MMS
message is sent through. MMS messages are sent through WAP,
whereas SMS messages are sent through global system for mobile
communications (GSM). Technological limitations of the mobile
phones such as small screen size, difficulty of use, and nonstan-
dardized WAP browsers also contributed to the slow takeoff

of MMS. However, mobile handheld devices have been transformed into pocket-sized mobile computers capable of providing improved computational power coupled with enlarged screens, touch-screens, and functional mini-keypads. Additionally, the promise of third-generation networks (3G) will dramatically enhance adoption of mobile multimedia service by increasing the speed of connectivity and lowering costs.

MMS messages allow mobile marketers to better customize marketing messages with the use of photos, illustrations, music, and video clips (see Exhibit 1.7).

Richer and more compelling content can be delivered to existing and potential customers via MMS (see Exhibit 1.8). Ringtones, both in the form of traditional mobile ringtones and MP3s, are delivered via MMS and are perceived as a means to make personal statements or of self-expression for consumers.

EXHIBIT 1.7 EXAMPLE OF A VIDEO MESSAGE

EXHIBIT 1.8 AN EXAMPLE OF AN MMS CAMPAIGN

The purpose of the campaign was to promote Renault Symbol just before the Autoshow exhibition. Target users were invited to participate in a short quiz about Renault Symbol via MMS to win tickets to the Autoshow. The return rate was 5 percent, and all tickets were given out within the first 20 minutes.

The Mobile Internet

The predominant communication protocol used to bring Internet-based content and advanced value-added services to mobile handheld devices was the wireless application protocol (WAP). WAP is a universal standard for a mobile application environment that mimics hypertext transport protocol (HTTP). Similar to Web sites, WAP sites are hosted on servers and are transmitted to mobile handheld devices using the same transmission protocol as Web sites, that is HTTP. Web sites are coded mainly using hypertext markup language (HTML), whereas WAP sites use wireless markup language (WML), based on extensible markup language (XML). Although WAP represented the birth of the mobile Internet, because of the lack of high-speed connection and its high cost, acceptance of WAP was not as widespread as it was predicted to be. WAP usage is charged by the duration of the connection, which consequently results in higher mobile phone charges.

General packet radio service (GPRS) is a radio technology for GSM networks that adds packet-switching protocols and offers the possibility for service providers to charge customers by the amount of data sent rather than connect time. GPRS uses a TCP/IP [TCP/IP is the common name for the set of communication protocols used for the Internet and similar networks: the Transmission Control Protocol (TCP) and the Internet Protocol (IP)] stack in the phone to send and receive data in high-speed packets just like the Internet. GPRS is an "always-on" system that connects the mobile device to the Internet, and it is the enabling technology behind today's mobile Internet application environment. GPRS is much faster than WAP because it is specifically designed to run on 3G networks. It is more efficient, easier to use, and cheaper for the user. The higher bandwidth version of GPRS is enhanced data rates for global evolution (EDGE). It provides an even higher-speed connection for bandwidth-hungry multimedia applications. Today, WAP, GPRS, and EDGE are the most widely used platforms for the delivery of mobile multimedia services and applications.

The services offered via mobile Internet can be classified into three categories:

1. *Commerce-based applications.* These mobile applications allow users to engage in commercial transactions on the

move. (e.g., mobile shopping, mobile banking, e-ticketing, and other interactive services provided by m-marketers).

2. *Content-based applications.* These mobile applications provide only information (e.g., downloads, news, traffic/weather/stock updates, services supporting users searching for online resources, and other time-sensitive and location-based services).

3. *Community-based applications.* These mobile applications allow users to interact with each other and establish social relationships (e.g., chat, e-mail, SMS messages, forum, and instant messages).

Mobile Internet sites represent a convenient channel for marketers to provide their customers with branded content that can be downloaded to their personal handheld devices. Branded mobile content does not only increase brand exposure, but it also reinforces brand communities as well. Today, many global brands have mobile Internet sites where their customers can download various types of branded mobile content to their handheld devices such as wallpapers, ringtones, music, videos, and games.

Designing Effective WAP Sites

WAP sites work best when their content is specifically tailored to address use context (such as the time and place the device is being used, the situation the user is in when using the device, motives for using the device, and so on) and limitations of mobile handsets (e.g., small screens and input/output difficulties). A WAP site designer should always keep in mind that users of WAP sites are on the move, seeking convenience and ease-of-use and that they will have little tolerance for waiting for things to load. Hence, the most important issue in WAP site design is the organization of the site structure. The most relevant information should always be in immediate reach, and users should always be able to return to the homepage with a single click. Navigational structure should be easy to understand, and actionable links should be easy to identify.

Since users will have little tolerance for long loading times, use of multiple screens instead of a single heavy content page is preferable. Furthermore, users should always be informed of what is happening in the background. Otherwise they may assume that there is something wrong with the connection and leave the WAP site.

To speed up loading and reduce possible interoperability problems (e.g., different renderings of various image formats in different handsets or size restrictions on older handsets), images should be used with caution. However, placement of images, icons, and fancy media substantially increase the visual aesthetics of mobile Internet sites. Therefore, the best strategy is to test the WAP site on a number of different handsets before the site is launched.

Mobile Portals

Proliferation of the mobile Internet gave birth to mobile portals, which aim to provide users with an all-inclusive solution for all their mobile Internet-related needs, such as e-mail, search, calendar, instant messaging, content downloads, and services from various providers (see Exhibit 1.9 for a screen shot of the mobile portal of Turkcell). Because of the input and navigational difficulties of mobile devices and the importance of convenience for mobile users, mobile portals may play a more significant role than traditional Internet portals. Today, most of the mobile operators have mobile portals, through which they hope to generate additional revenue and establish closer relationships with their existing customers. Through mobile portals, mobile operators can

1. Charge users additional subscription and usage fees.
2. Generate revenue from advertising.
3. Collect information about the preferences of their users and identify their navigational/behavioral patterns.
4. Collect user permission for mobile advertising.
5. Claim a portion of revenues generated by partnering with content or application providers, leveraging the portal's traffic.

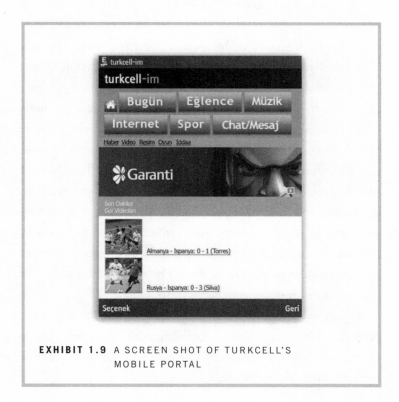

EXHIBIT 1.9 A SCREEN SHOT OF TURKCELL'S MOBILE PORTAL

Besides mobile operators, traditional Internet portals (e.g., AOL, Google, Yahoo!, and MSN) have also established mobile portals to leverage their existing brand image and customer base. In order to compete within their original line of services, they also need to create a mobile presence. Otherwise, their existing customers who are on the move may have no choice but to use mobile services provided by their rivals, which may eventually result in loss of the customer. Furthermore, not having a mobile presence may be perceived as failure of the brand to keep up with the latest technological trends, which may pose a significant threat to brand equity. The brand may lose its category membership to the cluster of cutting-edge technology brands. The existence of such pressures, when combined with the opportunities offered by mobile portals in maintaining a close relationship with customers, resulted in the establishment of many mobile portals, intensifying the competition for customer loyalty in the mobile environment. Today, various mass media companies, device manufacturers, consumer brands, mobile operators, financial organizations, traditional Internet portals, and several independent initiatives have well-established mobile portals. Therefore, to be able to compete and generate sustainable traffic, mobile portals need to offer their customers a compelling set of highly-personalized services and applications that are easy to use and fun. These must be at a reasonable price, and the content of the portal should be up to date and highly relevant for its target users.

Apart from their usefulness as customer relationship management or brand community building vehicles, mobile portals can also be used as an advertising medium for other mobile Internet sites. Some mobile Internet portals are sponsored by advertisers who place WAP links and banners that, if clicked, direct the user to the promoted mobile Internet sites (referred as the landing page). WAP banners and WAP links are very much similar to PC-based Internet banners, except that they need to be more compact because of the size and visibility constraints of mobile devices. Exhibit 1.10 includes examples of WAP banners taken from Turkcell-im, the mobile portal of the market leader mobile operator of Turkey, Turkcell, which had been visited by 2.5 million individual mobile users per month in 2010. Exhibit 1.11 shows a banner campaign for Pepsi.

EXHIBIT 1.10 EXAMPLES OF BANNERS TAKEN FROM TURKCELL-IM MOBILE PORTAL

EXHIBIT 1.11 A WAP BANNER CAMPAIGN FOR PEPSI

Theme: The banner directs the user to a WAP page designed to distribute branded wallpapers.

Interactive Voice Response

Interactive voice response (IVR) systems allow users to interact with an automated communications system over the phone. An IVR system prompts users with a prerecorded script. Then it requires a response from the user either orally or by pressing a touchtone key. It then supplies the user with information based on the responses given. IVR systems are typically used to service high call volumes, reduce cost, and improve the customer experience. Examples of typical IVR applications are: telephone banking, televoting, and credit card transactions. Some companies use IVR services to extend their business hours. Mobile operators use IVR systems to interact with subscribers in incentive-based marketing campaigns for the purpose of automated consumer data collection, market research, or promotion. Targeted users receive an automated call which seeks a response from the mobile user in the form of a marketing communication, and finally the user chooses his or her reward for participating (see Exhibit 1.12 for an example of an IVR marketing theme).

EXHIBIT 1.12 EXAMPLE OF AN IVR MARKETING THEME

Theme: A group of target consumers that consists of 15,000 people is informed of a campaign for Sana via IVR. Besides promoting the brand, the IVR campaign also revealed an approximate proportion of the target consumers who currently have Sana in their homes. Eighty percent of respondents have answered the call, of which 56 percent replied with an action.

Intro IVR Message: Hello! I am calling to inform you that the "Çat Kapı" [unexpected knock on the door] crew of Sana brand has set off on the road. Our teams will come to your city very soon and will visit many homes unexpectedly. We wanted to contact you in advance to find out if you had Sana in your kitchen or not. If you have Sana at home right now press 1, if you don't, press 2.

If the response is 1: Fantastic! A Sana "Çat Kapı" crew may knock on your door at any moment. Meanwhile, we would like to advise you to buy Sana if you have run out of it, because "Çat Kapı" teams reward kitchens where they find Sana. Surprise gifts await those housewives who use Sana. See you very soon.

If the response is 2: Nowadays, it would be wise if you always had Sana in your kitchen, because a Sana crew may knock on your door at any moment and ask to see Sana in your home. If you demonstrate that you would not give up the taste of Sana for anything else, you may win surprise gifts. Good luck. See you very soon...

Ringback Tone

A ringback tone (RBT) is the audible ringing sound that is heard on the telephone line by the calling party after dialing and prior to the call being answered. This tone is an indication for the calling party that a call is in progress and that the phone of the called party is ringing. In recent years the majority of mobile operators have launched personalized RBT service to their customers. Personalized ringback tones allow the customization of the ringback tone by the called party. The standard ringing sound is replaced with a clip of music or a voice recording. This is a feature of the network, not the phone. With this feature, callers hear an audio selection applied to the telephone line that has been previously determined by the called party.

Aforementioned mobile marketing tools can be utilized in an interactive combination to create innovative applications or advertising platforms that can even convert subscribers into advertisers of brands. See Exhibit 1.13 for an award-winning example of such applications, the TonlaKazan platform of Turkcell. Exhibit 1.14 shows another example of a successful m-marketing campaign.

EXHIBIT 1.13. TONE & WIN, AN AWARD-WINNING RINGBACK TONE ADVERTISING PLATFORM OF TURKCELL

Tone & Win, a ringback tone (RBT) personalization marketing scheme, is a platform that uses multiple tools of interactive mobile media such as RBT, mobile Internet, and IVR to turn sub-

scribers into advertising agents who are getting paid by prepaid minutes. Brands present their logos and jingles in the mobile Web site of Tone & Win. Then subscribers pick a brand from the mobile Web site that they wish to play its jingle to their friends when they call. They personalize their ringback tone with their favorite brand's jingle. Subscribers can easily keep track of how much prepaid minutes they won through IVR, mobile, or PC-based Internet. The operator charges the advertiser company on the basis of cost per listen, and only if the jingle is listened to for more than 5 seconds.

The innovativeness of the application lies in its ability to create a win-win position for all stakeholders. The users of the application not only win prepaid minutes but also personalize their mobile device with a jingle that they like or wish to be associated with. Furthermore, the advertisement jingle is played to the caller when his or her attention level is high and the source of the marketing communication happens to be a peer.

EXHIBIT 1.14. EXAMPLE OF AN M-MARKETING SCHEME THAT LEVERAGES RBT TO CREATE MOBILE WORD OF MOUTH

Theme: Participants won 10 free airtime units and immediately received a call from Seda Sayan, the celebrity of the campaign. The audio message varied according to the day of the week or stage of the promotion. This way the brand enjoyed genuine word of mouth, facilitated by consumers' thrill of receiving personalized calls from the celebrity. Furthermore, participants' ringback tones were automatically converted to Pepsi's jingle, as the awarded airtime units were positioned as "Tone&Win" units. The campaign not only turned participants into radio stations broadcasting the Pepsi jingle, but also facilitated introduction of Turkcell's Tone&Win platform to new users.

The campaign was a great success. Pepsi not only set a record in sales and market share, but also increased the participation rate of the housewives segment.

Mobile Games

Mobile games allow users to engage in interactive single-player or multiplayer games against other remote users regardless of time and location restrictions. There are a variety of game genres that are currently on the market ranging from simple time-killer puzzle games to more elaborate action adventure games. Mobile games can be either downloaded to the mobile handheld device as an application or played over an Internet portal. In either case mobile games can be used by a company for advertising or community building purposes. For example, King Kong was the most downloaded game in the United Kingdom in December 2005, which was used to advertise the movie and other related products. Similarly, The Asphalt Urban GT2, a multiplayer car racing game, was used as an advertising tool by car manufacturers to promote their models as dream cars (Salo and Karjaluoto, 2007). When a mobile game is specifically designed as an ad, the main source of revenue for the game developer comes from the advertiser instead of the downloading and playing fees charged to the end user.

Mobile games provide convenient entertainment for people on the move and provide an innovative means to promote products, brands, ideas, and services. More importantly, multiplayer games have the potential to foster community building by allowing interaction between game players; in other words, by providing a group of people a pleasant experience to share.

Mobile Payments

Mobile payment systems are suitable for many kinds of micropayments in the form of daily expenditures and virtual content. In a mobile payment plan, the mobile network operator assumes the responsibility for billing, similar to the role of a credit card provider. Their major value proposition is convenience. They basically replace the use of change and credit cards in routine micropayments and virtual content purchases such as Web site memberships or online content downloads. They are especially useful for targeting the expenditures of consumers who do not have credit cards, such as youngsters. Apart from online content purchases, several successful mobile payments systems have already been launched by various quick-service–oriented industries such as parking lots (e.g., ispark), public transportation (e.g., Octopus), toll booths (e.g., E-ZPass and FasTrak), gas stations (e.g., Exxon Mobil and Speedpass), fast-food restaurants (e.g., McDonald's), retail vending machines (e.g., Sonera Mobile Pay), and ski resort ticketing (e.g., SKIDATA) (Ondrus and Pigneur, 2006). See Exhibits 1.15 and 1.16 for examples of mobile payment plans.

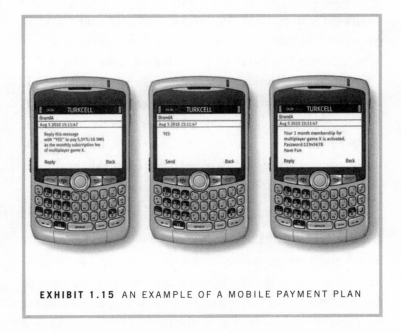

EXHIBIT 1.15 AN EXAMPLE OF A MOBILE PAYMENT PLAN

EXHIBIT 1.16 AN EXAMPLE OF A MOBILE PAYMENT PLAN

Ispark, the private company that operates and manages all the public parking lots in Istanbul, Turkey, has launched a mobile fee collection plan in collaboration with Turkcell. The system is permission-based and requires a one-time-only registration via SMS. After explicit opt-in, Turkcell subscribers can utilize the system by sending an SMS to a specified number with the location code written at the Ispark signboard at the parking lot. The system replies with a confirmation message. Ispark workers can monitor the receipt of the parking fee via their hand terminals. The system provides convenience to subscribers by removing the necessity of carrying and dealing with change in parking lot payments. Not only does it provide a reliable and convenient way to pay for such a routine expenditure, but it also provides further customer service by sending a notification SMS to the customer before the parking ticket expires.

Location-Based Services

A unique feature of the mobile medium is that it allows the mobile marketer to know the current position of the target user with great precision and therefore adapt the marketing impulse accordingly. Location-based services (LBSs) are enabled by geolocation technologies such as the global positioning system (GPS) or cell of origin (COO). Leveraging these technologies, mobile marketers use the location and other information based on consumer databases to provide personalized mobile services that capture both consumer preferences and the context that the user is in. Some examples include time- and location-sensitive special offers, timely teasers, and warning notifications. Such mobile marketing messages offer the unprecedented opportunity of increasing contextual relevance of the message, hence increasing effectiveness of the marketing impulse.

Apart from providing new strength to push type mobile marketing messages as discussed above, localization technology also provides valuable pull-type mobile services to mobile subscribers. These applications include, "What's near me?" services allowing identification of nearby buyers and sellers, route guidance, roadside assistance, and weather/traffic information (see Exhibit 1.17). Location-aware information may be particularly useful in special situations, such as navigating in unfamiliar environments, when looking for a specific service, in emergency situations, accessibility information for disabled users, and speech-based guidance for the visually impaired (Barnes, 2003; Kaasinen, 2003).

A widely utilized technology for providing location-specific marketing, without using a global positioning system, is cell broadcasting (CBC). A cell broadcast is a technology that allows a text or binary message to be distributed to all mobile terminals

EXHIBIT 1.17 EXAMPLES OF M-MARKETING CAMPAIGNS THAT LEVERAGE LOCATION INFORMATION

Akbank, a Turkish bank, launched a location-based campaign in which the company promised its cardholders to pay back 10 percent of the credit card (Wings) expenditures they incurred abroad. Leveraging location-based services, Akbank identified Wings card holders who were abroad and sent permission-based SMS messages informing these specific customers about the campaign. The campaign has successfully increased the Wings usage rate abroad.

Leveraging location-based services, Garanti Bank, another Turkish bank, provides mobile users with the addresses of its branches and ATMs within the 4 km radius around the mobile user. All the mobile user has to do is to click the related link in the mobile Internet site of Garanti Bank.

connected to a set of cells or towers. Cell broadcasting enables one to many geographically focused messages, based on simultaneous delivery of mobile messages to multiple users in a specified area. CBC messages are not recorded in the mobile handset; they are shown to the user for a short period of time and then disappear. In a cellular network there exist 64,000 broadcast channels which make it possible for an operator to offer many services on different channels that use the basic broadcast technology. To receive a broadcast message the mobile subscriber must tune into that broadcast channel. Hence CBC message delivery is ultimately controlled by the user. Most of the recent mobile handset models do have cell broadcast capability, and most of the major global mobile network operators have already deployed CBC technology. For example, Turkcell delivers sports-related notifications through CBC channel 55, and its own promotions through channel 1. There are currently 8.5 million Turkcell subscribers whose CBC channel 55 is open and 9.5 million subscribers whose CBC channel 1 is open.

An improved version of CBC is a service booster, which enables the delivery of a cell broadcasted message to the hand terminal without the requirement of manual activation of the service by the user. The channel can be turned on remotely. Therefore, service booster messages are delivered only to subscribers who have already given their explicit permission to receive such messages. Service booster messages may be interactive and contain enhanced text-based graphics. Examples of location-based services appear in Exhibits 1.18 and 1.19.

EXHIBIT 1.18 EXAMPLES OF LOCATION-BASED SERVICES

Theme: Where's the nearest store that carries a particular brand?

Turkcell uses CBC service booster technology to provide subscribers with the information they are looking for. For example, when a user texts a brand name to 7777, Turkcell responds with the location information about the nearest store of that brand. The message also includes a link that provides the user with a map of the requested location.

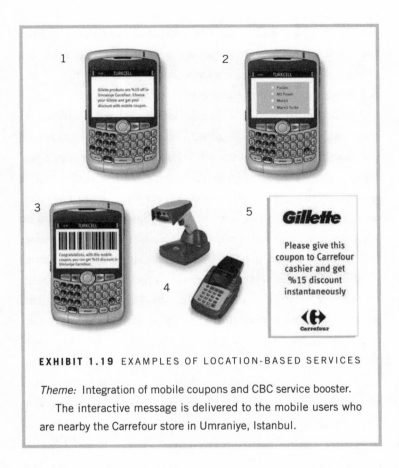

EXHIBIT 1.19 EXAMPLES OF LOCATION-BASED SERVICES

Theme: Integration of mobile coupons and CBC service booster.

The interactive message is delivered to the mobile users who are nearby the Carrefour store in Umraniye, Istanbul.

Mobile TV

There are two forms of mobile TV: streamed mobile TV and broadcast mobile TV. Streamed mobile TV is the most common form at present. It uses the mobile network operator's (MNO) network (2G/2.5G or 3G) to stream TV content to mobile hand-held devices. It is primarily unicast, meaning that each recipient has a dedicated network transmission. The primary problem with unicast streaming is that the network could quickly become overwhelmed when a large number of users simultaneously try to stream TV. Therefore, streamed mobile TV may not be the best service to use for popular events such as live sports events.

In broadcast mobile TV such capacity-related problems do not exist because of the multicast design. Digital multimedia broadcasting occurs over an overlay network, which uses a frequency that is separate from the normal carrier traffic and is specifically designed to prevent or alleviate the streaming video congestion on stream carriers' networks. Since broadcast mobile TV does not require the existence of mobile network operators in the supply chain, it poses a serious threat to the dominating position of mobile network operators in the mobile value chain. In order to take preventative action for this critical problem, mobile network operators have heavily invested in building necessary infrastructure in their coverage areas, and they have purchased broadcast frequency rights from local regulatory agencies.

However, a number of mobile device manufacturers started to introduce new mobile handhelds that are capable of receiving analog and digital terrestrial TV with relatively low power consumption. Analog and digital terrestrial TV can be aired free. If these devices become widely available and popular, streamed and broadcast mobile TV services would be faced with a huge marketing problem. Although wide adoption of payment-based mobile TV is not expected in the near future, there will always be a market for some video-on-demand form of premium TV that is delivered to mobile handsets. Whether streamed or broadcast, content providers are in the best strategic position to take advantage of mobile TV, because without them there would be nothing to watch.

Although the necessary infrastructure exists, mobile TV has not been launched in Turkey yet. One of the biggest risk factors for launching mobile TV is estimating consumer demand. Will it be regarded as merely an interesting technological innovation, or will it become a mobile application that would be used on a regular basis?

Mobile Tagging

Mobile tagging is the process of providing data on mobile devices through the use of data on a two-dimensional bar code which are designed to be read by a mobile device with a built-in camera. Mobile tagging makes it possible for users to connect to a mobile Web site with a simple "point and click" of their mobile handsets without entering long URLs by hand or scrolling through Web content that's not relevant to them.

Although initially designed and used to track parts in manufacturing, two-dimensional bar codes are now used in a much broader context, including both commercial tracking applications and convenience-oriented applications aimed at mobile phone users, especially in the field of mobile marketing. Users with a handset that has a built-in camera and is equipped with the correct reader software can scan the image of a particular mobile tag, which would cause the phone's browser to launch and be redirected to the programmed URL. This process is unique in terms of providing quick, precise, and customer-driven access to information. In order to deliver its value proposition, mobile tags must be well placed, highly visible, and easy to interact with.

Mobile tags may appear in brochures, in magazines, in newspapers, on signs, on buses, on billboards, on business cards, in store displays, on commercial packaging, or with practically any object that users might need information about. Marketers may use mobile tagging to provide additional information about their products (e.g., the nutrient content in packaged food) or events (e.g., concerts, parties, conferences, etc.) to facilitate direct downloads (e.g., branded mobile content) and to provide easy-to-use links to specific mobile sites. Furthermore, mobile tags allow services like saving data automatically in the contact list of a mobile handset by scanning a 2D bar code printed on a business card. Such tagging of objects with this technology created a new layer of linkages between the physical and electronic worlds, which positioned mobile tags as the hyperlinks of the physical world (see Exhibit 1.20 for examples of mobile tags and Exhibit 1.21 for an example of a mobile marketing campaign that uses mobile tags).

While software developers and marketers are launching their own experiments with the use of 2D bar codes, widespread adoption of mobile tags is likely to depend on the establishment of a universal standard for generating and reading 2D mobile bar codes. Because of the absence of a standard code, most of the software available on the market cannot identify bar codes apart from their own proprietary codes. On the other hand, there are several readers that were created to read nonproprietary open source codes, such as the QR code and the data matrix.

Although mobile tagging technology is still relatively new in the United States and Europe, thanks to DoCoMo's support for the technology, it is already very popular in Japan. In Japan

EXHIBIT 1.20 EXAMPLES OF MOBILE TAGS

it is possible to find a mobile tag on almost anything that has a suitable surface that allows placement of a 2D bar code. Japanese entrepreneurs pushed the idea and created ingenious applications of mobile tagging technology (see Exhibit 1.22).

EXHIBIT 1.21 AN EXAMPLE OF A MOBILE MARKETING CAMPAIGN THAT USES MOBILE TAGS

KidRobot, a New York-based company that makes limited edition toys and clothing, launched a massive scavenger hunt for adults around New York City in August 2009. People who wanted to play got clues that would lead them to a hidden 2D mobile bar code placed on a single poster somewhere in the city. Those who successfully tracked down the bar code and scanned it got prizes. The toys given away were from the "Dunny" collection, and so the campaign was called the "Dunny Hunt."

Fans of KidRobot could get their clues via Twitter, the KidRobot newsletter, or in any KidRobot store. KidRobot provided full details on how to download and install the scanner that is needed to read the mobile tag. The ones who found the poster and scanned the bar code were entered into a drawing to win a complete set of Dunny toys. The first person to scan the tag every day also won a prize. This imaginative promotion campaign successfully appealed to Kidrobot's fan base in a very fun, exciting, and progressive way.

Embedded Mobile Devices

Embedded mobile devices allow machine-to-machine communication with the ultimate aim of enhancing customer satisfaction. Preventative action, instead of reactive customer service,

EXHIBIT 1.22 AN IMAGINATIVE MOBILE TAGGING APPLICATION

An imaginative Japanese entrepreneur applied mobile tagging to tombs. Once the 2D bar code is scanned by a visitor of the tomb, his or her mobile handset serves as an electronic scrapbook, providing a means for visitors to post and view different items that reflect on the life of their departed loved one, such as photos, quotes, and memories. Though the concept seems a bit weird, the application is ingenious in terms of its power to facilitate sharing of user-generated content.

is possible with the help of the smart mobile devices that are embedded in products. These smart devices monitor the functioning of the product and notify the company about faulty parts. They provide maintenance before the faulty part breaks the entire machine. Such an action prevents the customer from going through a negative experience related to the product. Another possible use of embedded devices in the domain of customer service is automatically signaling a control center when an urgent situation occurs, such as when a car crashes or an alarm goes off.

Other Marketing-Related Uses of Mobile Technologies

Integration of mobile technologies into enterprise information systems provides the opportunity for improving internal communication and efficiency. There are two types of mobile business solutions: The first is the set of applications that provides real-time information for field force employees, and the second is the use of embedded mobile devices that provides tracking of supply chain operations. For the mobile workforce, immediate access to information stored in various kinds of corporate data repositories is very important. Mobile employees need billing, contact, technical, operational, and market-related information to enhance real-time customer service.

On the other hand, the headquarters needs timely data input from the field force to be able to assess current information about customers, inventory, work orders, work schedules, and other important data. Delayed data entry into corporate databases impedes an organization's ability to manage its supply chain and thus decreases its market responsiveness. Integration of the mobile medium with enterprise resource planning systems will leverage the existing infrastructure to maximize its value.

Mobile Social Networking

The success of social networking sites (e.g., Facebook, Twitter, MySpace, FriendFeed) shows that people, especially young people, love sharing social media content. They share videos, pictures, stories, jokes, comments, critiques, games, articles, profiles, preferences, and even advertisements with their peers through these online platforms. People enjoy broadcasting their real-time whereabouts and status. Through mobile components of Web sites and programs (also called widgets) designed to minimize the interface of those sites to fit small screens and maximize their usability on tiny devices, these social networking sites entered mobile space. Since mobile handsets are transformed into constant companions that no one can ever afford to leave behind, they provide the perfect channel for social sharing. In most cases the value of social content is directly linked to its timeliness. As the information gets older, it loses its value. The mobile medium offers the "immediacy" that cannot be provided by PCs.

With their mobile devices, people do not have to wait until they get home to tell their friends about their day, criticize the movie they just saw, or share a wonderful picture they took with their built-in cameras. Furthermore, widgets downloaded to mobile handsets facilitate this process. It is expected that virtually every online social network application is going to have a mobile component over the next few years. With the current software that is available, interactions within mobile social networks are not limited to exchanging simple text messages on a one-to-one basis but are constantly evolving toward the sophisticated interactions of virtual communities. In most mobile communities, members can now create their own profiles, participate in chat rooms, create chat rooms, make friends, engage in private conversations, play multiplayer games, share various types of multimedia content, and interact with the content that is generated by other users (e.g., comment on any post) by using their mobile handsets. Some applications allow users to view an up-to-date map of friends' locations, collected through the global positioning system (GPS) available in most phones. A good mobile social networking application should let a user easily view, manage, and post to their streams and interact with content on their stream.

Today, mobile social networking is on the rise, and there is fierce competition among rival applications in the market. Although many of them provide mo re or less the same features, the latest trend is to incorporate geolocation information in user profiles. For instance, an iPhone application called 3banana lets users tag map locations with virtual, Post-it–like notes and share those observations with friends via Twitter, Facebook, or the user's own 3banana network of contacts. Recently, Google launched its location-based program, Latitude. It allows users to let their locations on Google Maps be known, and it lets them track friends and family who have also opted in. Yahoo! also launched a similar application, Friends on Fire, which works with Facebook to let contacts there know where they are. Loopt is another pioneer of the genre, which shows users where their friends are located and what they are doing via detailed, interactive maps on their mobile phones. Loopt users can also share location updates, geotagged photos, and comments with anyone in their mobile address book or on their online social networks. The giants of online social networking, Facebook and MySpace, are allowing third-party software makers to integrate their applications with their platforms.

Some social networking applications specialize in specific media types. For instance, Flickr allows users to post photos shot with their mobiles onto the Flickr site with one click. Some of them act as an aggregator of one's social media (see Exhibit 1.23). For instance, FriendFeed brings all the self-generated social media content (from Facebook, Flickr, YouTube, Twitter, and blogs) onto one site and allows the user to share that content with anyone else who also uses FriendFeed, and see a stream of other's social media.

Mobile social networking represents a new source of revenue for the entire mobile value chain. For mobile network operators, mobile social networking means increased data traffic

EXHIBIT 1.23 SOCIAL LIFE, A MOBILE SOCIAL NETWORKING AGGREGATOR

Orange UK has launched Social Life, a mobile social networking aggregator that displays users' activity on Facebook, MySpace, and Bebo on a single screen. Social Life is accessible from Orange's mobile Internet portal Orange World. It basically allows customers to view and post updates and get in touch with friends and family across all three social networks at the same time through a single log in. Users of Social Life can upload photos, broadcast their status, and keep track of friends' feeds from all three social networks. They can also receive notifications such as messages, events, pokes, and friend requests, and interact with others. The system is ultimately permission-based, such that users have full control over which information they provide to each of their social networks. Social Life also allows users to set up and send free text alerts for social activities.

rates and air time. Since sharing social media content requires increased air time, it also encourages users to buy unlimited data plans. For content providers, mobile social networking applications and platforms provide an excellent environment to unleash viral campaigns. Viral campaigns require campaign- and target-specific multimedia content (e.g., branded videos, branded wallpapers, ringtones, music, stories, and news) to be generated, which increases demand for the services of content providers. Finally, since social networking applications group users into highly targeted categories, such as art lovers, graduates of a college, fans of a sports club, or people located in a particular area, owners of such applications might be able to charge advertisers a premium.

According to future prospects of industry visionaries, a few years from now mobile devices will help people remember details of people they know and meet new people for dating, business, and friendship. A day will come when people will be able to see profile information such as name, dating status, and résumé information about other people in an area, depending on privacy settings. The information that is available would be relevant to the context. For instance, people may broadcast their curriculum vitae from Linkedin in a business meeting or a conference, and their dating status from Facebook in a bar. Users will be able to scroll through nearby users and set filters for various attributes. Such applications will be the ultimate layer of linkage between the virtual world and the physical world. They will have a tremendous impact on conventional socializing practices.

Advantages of Mobile Marketing over Traditional Media

- Measures of success are more detailed, reliable, and easier to track.
- Allows live campaign measurement and tracking.
- SMS marketing is extremely cost-effective.
- Allows ultimate one-to-one marketing: since high levels of personal data can be made available to mobile operators and service providers about customers, advanced targeting and finer control over dissemination of information is possible in mobile marketing.
- Highly interactive.
- Has immediate impact: allows instant customer response.
- Allows role/situation congruence of the message: more likely to be effective.
- Allows situational targeting: advertising will appear only to those users who are at a particular place or attending a particular event.
- Response rates are generally over 10 percent.
- Mobile advertisements can be stored in the memory of handhelds: reduces the cognitive load placed on the consumer and acts as a reminder in the future.
- Allows immediate sharing of marketing messages among peers: has a strong viral element.

2

Unique Value Propositions

The Difference of the Mobile Medium

It is important to understand which aspects of the mobile medium are influential in determining which mobile services end users want. Doing so enables marketers to develop applications and services that highlight those aspects of the mobile medium in order to improve their offerings' value proposition. Consumers evaluate offerings according to their perception of the value of the offering. Consumers generally assess an offering by comparing it with alternatives. Therefore, the decision to use mobile services will be based on the perceived relative advantage of the mobile medium with respect to alternative media. This elicits the ultimate question: What makes mobile medium significantly different from its alternatives?

The mobile medium is significantly superior to any other media in terms of ubiquity, convenience, personalization, and localization (Clarke, 2001).

Ubiquity

The mobile medium is unprecedentedly ubiquitous because it allows omnipresence of information and continual access to commerce. Mobile technology enables consumers to receive and send information and perform transactions virtually anywhere at any time. Since consumers derive utilitarian value from efficient and timely service delivery in general (Childers et al., 2001), it can be claimed that mobile devices are especially useful in providing utilitarian value. Further, the ubiquitous nature of mobile marketing provides value to users by fulfilling time-critical needs (Anckar and D'Incau, 2002). For instance, mobile content services allow for the delivery of time-sensitive information (often sponsored by brands) on certain topics that the user recognizes as urgent (stock-related alerts for traders and investors, weather-related alerts for surfers, etc.). The value of such information is often linked with its timely use, therefore the always-on connectivity of the mobile medium makes mobile marketing particularly effective in this respect. It should be noted that the perceived value of the mobile medium will definitely differ for different kinds of consumer groups. For instance, younger users do not necessarily seek utilitarian value; instead they use the mobile medium primarily for socializing and entertainment.

Convenience

The mobile medium is exceptionally convenient. Mobile devices are always with the user and are always connected. This convenience is the key advantage of the mobile medium for consumers. It provides value to consumers by fulfilling efficiency needs and ambitions (Anckar and D'Incau, 2002), such as the need to increase productivity during dead periods of the day (e.g., while stuck in traffic, waiting in line in a grocery store, waiting for a bus) when the consumer is unable to access the PC-based Internet. Mobile information services allow consumers to receive information even when they are engaged in another activity, such as meeting people or travelling. A variety of mobile services allows users to conduct transactions on the move. Such aspects of mobile marketing drive consumer demand for mobile content services, which consequently makes the mobile medium an increasingly attractive channel for sponsorships and advertisements. It has been found that usefulness is not the top concern for mobile Internet adopters; instead the mobile Internet is used primarily for convenience (Kim et al., 2007; Mahatanankoon et al., 2005). Therefore, increasing perceived convenience should be an important agenda for mobile application developers. Perceived convenience is the result of perceived connection of quality and perceived ease of use. Mobile marketers should aim at

1. Improving customers' belief in the marketers' ability to provide a connection between the mobile device and the Internet that is satisfying in terms of speed and reliability.
2. Decreasing the perceived level of effort in engaging with the mobile service.

Personalization

Mobile phones are very personal in nature. Most of the time, answering someone else's mobile phone or taking a look at its stored contents is socially unacceptable. Therefore, mobile marketing provides an unprecedented opportunity to control the dissemination of information in the market, and it is an ideal tool for one-to-one marketing. Thanks to the technological capabilities of the mobile infrastructure and handheld devices, mobile marketers can design effective individually tailored message content that can include graphics, text, videos, and interactive components and then transmit the message to the target consumer with great precision. Personalization makes marketing messages increasingly relevant for the target consumer, and hence it is one of the most important factors affecting consumers' attitude toward mobile advertising.

Successful personalization is possible only with the help of effective databases and data-mining techniques. The most widely utilized mobile personalization algorithms use traditional user characteristics and device/channel characteristics as input. User characteristics include knowledge, goals, background, experience, demographics, personality traits, expressed preferences, and prior behavioral records. Device/channel characteristics refer to the capabilities of the device the target user has or the channel in use, which determines the technical aspects of message design. Behavioral records include prior navigational, transactional, and response data. A more innovative personalization scheme may incorporate visual attention, cognitive and emotional processing parameters, and learning styles to generate a more complete and comprehensive user profile (Germanakos et al., 2008). Although personalization of services is one of the founding pillars of the PC-based Internet as well, the importance of personalization is amplified in mobile marketing because of the technological limitations of the user interface of mobile devices, such as small screen size and difficulties in navigational ergonomics. The messages that are delivered to mobile devices are usually regarded as intrusive; thus the ability of the mobile marketing message in grabbing user attention and in not being considered spam is directly related to its relevance to the user and to the situation the user is in.

Personalization of the mobile content is also used within mobile campaigns to reinforce customer experience and increase brand exposure. For instance, Algida, during its mobile SMS campaign in which it rewarded customers with a test drive on the Formula One runway in England, provided customers with a personalized wallpaper in which the name of the mobile user was put on the front of the helmet of the F1 driver. Similarly, Pepsi reinforced its brand image by providing its customers with branded mobile content such as melodies, wallpaper, and mobile games.

Localization

Global positioning technologies allow the location of the mobile consumer to be determined. By leveraging this technology, marketers are able to transmit their personalized messages to their target consumers with great precision at the right location, when it is most needed. The ability to include contextual information in the personalization scheme is a distinctive feature of the mobile medium and is not possible in any other existing media. The relevance of the message (with respect to both preferences and the situation the user is in) is very valuable for consumers in helping in situations that require instant decision making. Knowledge of a discount in a nearby store that sells favorite brands is very valuable for a consumer. Such messages can guide consumers and may result in impulsive behavior in low-involvement situations.

Applications that manifest localization of the value proposition include time- and location-sensitive special offers, roadside assistance, "What's near me?" services allowing identification of nearby buyers and sellers, route guidance, road pricing, and weather or traffic information. Location-aware information may be especially useful in special situations, such as when consumers are navigating in unfamiliar environments, when they're looking for a specific service, in emergency situations, accessibility information for disabled users, and speech-based guidance for the visually impaired (Kaasinen, 2003).

Theories That Mobile Consumer Research Dwells On

The next chapter introduces a model for a successful mobile marketing strategy, which is based on the summary of findings of the mobile consumer behavior research stream. Therefore, before presenting the model, it would be of value to provide a brief overview of several fundamental theories that the mobile consumer behavior research stream is based on.

Many consumer behavior models dwell on the theory of reasoned action (TRA) (Fishbein and Ajzen, 1975). TRA proposes that the most significant determinant of actual consumer behavior is the intention of the consumer to perform a behavior, which is a function of attitude toward behavior and subjective norms. Ajzen (1985) revised TRA and included a third determinant of behavioral intention—perceived behavioral control—in his theory of planned behavior (TPB).

The technology acceptance model (TAM) is another derivation of TRA, by Davis (1989), which originally aimed at explaining individuals' adoption of traditional technology in an organizational setting. TAM asserts that all influences of external variables on behavior are mediated by usefulness and ease of use. However, adopters and users of new information and communications technology (ICT) are not mere technology users in an organizational setting, but they also play the role of a service consumer. Therefore, many authors augmented TAM to explain human behavior in a consumption context. The most prominent extension (TAM2) was proposed by Venkatesh and Davis (2000), who added social influence processes and cognitive instrumental processes to the original model.

Since consumption of mobile services is driven by both utilitarian and nonutilitarian motives, several authors extended TAM and TPB to include nonutilitarian motives (e.g., enjoyment, fun-seeking, status, fashion, and entertainment) which were reported in studies from the uses and gratification research. For example, Kim, Chan, and Gupta (2007) proposed a value-based adoption model of the mobile Internet as shown in Figure 2.1.

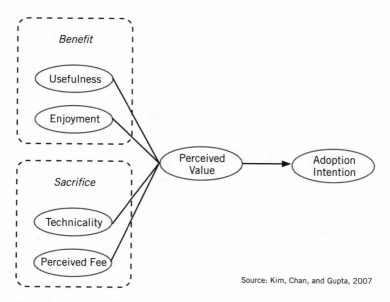

Source: Kim, Chan, and Gupta, 2007

FIGURE 2.1 VALUE-BASED ADOPTION MODEL OF THE MOBILE INTERNET

Innovation diffusion theory (IDT), proposed by Rogers (1983), is another well-known theory used for relevant information technology (IT) and information systems (IS) research. The central research issue of IDT is how an innovation is communicated through certain channels, over time, among the members of a social system. IDT includes five significant innovation characteristics: relative advantage, compatibility, complexity, trialability, and observables, of which only the relative advantage, compatibility, and complexity are found to be consistently related to innovation adoption in the field of information technologies. Relative advantage and complexity are quite similar to perceived usefulness and perceived ease of use, respectively. Compatibility is the degree to which the innovation is perceived to be consistent with the consumers' previous experiences, values, and needs. All the aforementioned models are similar in some constructs and can be used to supplement one another. For instance, Wu and Wang (2005) integrated TAM2 with IDT and two additional variables (cost and perceived risk) to model acceptance of mobile commerce in business-to-consumer (B2C) context. The constructs of perceived ease of use, perceived usefulness, behavioral intention to use, and actual use were adopted from TAM2. Compatibility was elicited from IDT. The model is shown in Figure 2.2.

In fact, because of inherent characteristics of the mobile medium, a comprehensive understanding of mobile consumer behavior requires an integrative approach that considers the end user as a technology user, a service consumer, and a network member (Pedersen, Methlie, and Thorbjørnsen, 2002). Therefore, all relevant models available in the literature should be applied in the mobile context to capture all emotional, cognitive, social, and cultural issues. Market research in pursuit of

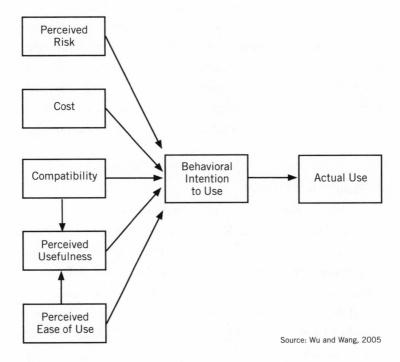

Source: Wu and Wang, 2005

FIGURE 2.2 USER ACCEPTANCE OF MOBILE COMMERCE

explaining patterns of mobile consumer behavior should encompass various constructs taken from all the aforementioned models in order to produce meaningful and useful input for strategy development in a mobile marketing campaign.

Codes of Conduct

There are several organizations worldwide that provide guidelines for the use of the mobile medium for marketing purposes (e.g., the Mobile Marketing Association and the Institute of

Practitioners in Advertising). These guidelines are advisory in nature and serve as industry self-regulations aimed at protecting consumers and their privacy, ultimately ensuring the success and integrity of the mobile content business. They also provide hints for best practices. Mobile marketers should be familiar with these guidelines in order to be aware of regulatory requirements and possible social and ethical consequences of their actions.

Consumer Privacy

Consumer privacy has two aspects in the mobile marketing context: freedom of choice and confidentiality. Freedom of choice refers to the right to privacy of the consumers, which is protected by permission-based marketing (discussed below). Confidentiality refers to the privacy and security of consumer information collected through mobile marketing campaigns. Codes of conduct launched by the Mobile Marketing Association requires mobile marketers to implement adequate technical, physical, and administrative procedures to protect user information from unauthorized use, alteration, disclosure, distribution, or access. Consumers' perception regarding the commitment of the mobile marketer to keeping consumer information private increases trust, which in turn significantly improves consumers' willingness to accept and engage in mobile marketing initiated by the mobile marketer.

Permission

A mobile phone is an intimate object that is part of an individual's personal sphere. Uninvited messages may be viewed as intrusions into the personal sphere. Intrusiveness refers to feelings of resentment, avoidance, and irritation that result from unexpected exposure to advertisements (Godin, 1999) and is related to the utility and expectedness of the interruption (Li, Edwards, and Lee, 2002). Therefore, factors that may mitigate intrusiveness include permission, message relevance, and inclusion of incentives (Krishnamurthy, 2000). The strategies that are pursued by mobile marketers related to these factors are permission-based marketing, personalization, and incentive-based marketing.

Explicit consumer permission is not only necessary for ethical reasons but is also critical for the acceptance and success of mobile marketing. Specifically, since an individual is usually targeted by several brands that deliver mobile advertising messages frequently, without explicit permission mobile marketing messages are at best ineffective and at worst could reduce brand equity by causing resentment and irritation (Barwise and Strong, 2002). On the other hand, explicit permission results in perceived user control which increases the likelihood of positive feelings and confidence about the outcome of engaging in any kind of activity. Perceived user control has a significant effect on consumers' attitudes toward mobile marketing and their willingness to receive mobile advertising messages.

User opt-in and ease of opt-out are the two crucial components of permission-based mobile marketing. User opt-in refers to explicit action taken by the user in order to accept messages that are from specific brands or related to specific causes. Users can opt-in through an online/offline survey, by sending an SMS, or by replying to an automated voice service. The essential issue is that opt-in messages should be clear, easy to understand, and explicit. Codes of conduct launched by the Institute of Practitioners in Advertising recommend that mobile marketers should request that the target audience text a word (such as yes) as a clear confirmation of opt-in. Ease of opt-out refers to the ease of getting out of the service. The information regarding how to unsubscribe from the service should be in immediate reach, clear, and explicit.

Perceived user control can be further enhanced by allowing the user to choose the timing of mobile messages, the number of mobile advertising messages, and the content of those messages (Carroll et al., 2007). Control over the timing, frequency, and content of the mobile marketing messages should further improve consumers' attitude toward the received messages and increase their willingness to engage with interactive messages.

Handling of Adult Content

Mobile devices are usually used by a single individual and can be highly personal. This makes the identities of mobile users more recognizable when compared to the users of the PC-based Internet. Hence, it is possible for mobile operators to limit access to adult content by installing age verification procedures. Mobile operators can block the distribution of and access to adult content for underage users. Adult content includes promotion and sale of alcohol, cigarettes, betting and gambling, and pornographic content such as text-based sex jokes and chatting, moan-tones in the form of screams, moans and groans, erotic images, videos, and games. Adult content has traditionally generated substantial revenue through a variety of entertainment media like magazines, the Internet, television, and videos. If suggested actions are taken, the mobile industry has the potential to become the first properly regulated channel for adult entertainment. In reality, different regulations apply in different countries, and operators enforce widely different policies for handling adult content all over the world.

Marketing to Children

The high penetration of mobile devices among minors creates serious risks of over-consumption and access to inappropriate content. This fact increases the responsibility of mobile marketers to be cautious when planning their mobile marketing campaigns. Content that may be harmful to children (e.g., photos illustrating violence, promoting being underweight, or pornographic content) must be distributed selectively, and marketers should refrain from appealing to children in promoting products. Appealing to adults through manipulation and exploitation of children's wants and desires is extremely unethical and presents an important consumer policy issue. Therefore, mobile marketers must obtain verifiable parental consent before communicating with minors.

Players in the Mobile Value Chain

The rapid proliferation of mobile technologies and the increasing penetration rate of smart phones and handheld computers have fueled the demand for enhanced digital services that provide entertainment and efficiency on the move. As a result, a brand-new economic ecosystem, called the mobile ecosystem, has quickly flourished to capitalize on the growing business potential of the mobile medium. The mobile ecosystem involves a number of players in a chain of value-adding activities that terminates with the customer (depicted in Figure 2.3, on page 64). The players of the mobile value chain are:

- ◉ *Network operators.* Companies that provide the infrastructure for mobile communications, including transportation, transmission, and switching for voice and data. These companies include major telecommunications players such as AT&T, NTT DoCoMo, T-Mobile, Orange, Turkcell, and Vodafone. Network operators route mobile transmissions, bill mobile end users, and collect revenue. Some mobile network operators are directly involved in the design and implementation of mobile marketing campaigns. Furthermore, mobile network operators organize conferences, workshops, and seminars in order to educate the market about the unique benefits of the mobile medium and facilitate the adoption of mobile marketing practices. Mobile marketing practices represent a new source of revenue for mobile operators.

- ◉ *Mobile Virtual Network Operators (MVNOs).* Companies that do not own a licensed frequency spectrum like a traditional carrier but rather resell services under their own brand name using the network of another mobile operator. MVNOs lower operational costs for mobile operators and build brands and relationships with consumers that could potentially threaten brand equity of traditional carriers over the long term.

- ◉ *Content providers.* These are the companies that develop digital rich content for the mobile medium. Examples of mobile content include ringtones, logos, videos, music, pictures, news, financial information, interactive guides, directories, Java applications, and games.

- ◉ *Advertising/media agencies.* Advertising agencies are the companies that are specialized in design and implementation of advertising campaigns. They serve brands by providing their expertise in advertising by generating and launching the advertising campaign and coordinating the rest of the value chain. Mobile marketing represents a new line in the media inventories of these companies, which complements other media while addressing advertiser companies' need for accountability. Because of its inherent characteristics, mobile marketing also provides a unique way of differentiating a brand.

⊙ *Aggregators.* Aggregators stand between content providers and network operators and provide several key value-added services. Through these companies, content providers gain access to major content providers, and, conversely, instead of dealing with many small content providers, network operators simplify their business by dealing with only few aggregators in order to offer all the available content to their customers. Aggregators create further value by providing digital rights management services and settling payment issues between its clients.

⊙ *Mobile marketing agencies.* The complex and highly competitive nature of the mobile world gave birth to specialized companies that design and implement mobile marketing campaigns, and provide advisory services to other players in the mobile value chain.

⊙ *Advertiser companies/brands.* All kinds of organizations that use the mobile channel for internal and external communication with their stakeholders. Mobile marketing is appealing to advertiser brands because it represents a cost-effective, direct, and personal communication channel, which produces high response rates, allowing for real-time response rate measurement.

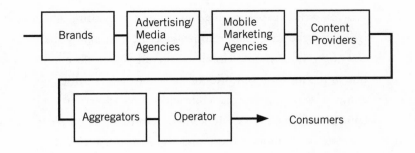

FIGURE 2.3 PLAYERS IN THE MOBILE VALUE CHAIN

Revenue and Business Models

Mobile operators have three main revenue models for mobile marketing practices. The first model is "pay per use," which is based on charging users for discrete uses of mobile services such as premium SMS, downloads of information, media, and applications or purchase of mobile Internet time. The second revenue model is "sponsored services," in which mobile services are offered free to users, but an advertisement is placed in the user interface (mobile Web site, SMS/MMS, or any kind of entertainment content). These kinds of mobile services are sponsored by the advertising company, and the revenue is collected from the advertising company on the basis of pricing model used. The final revenue model is "revenue sharing" between content providers and mobile operators. In revenue sharing models, the mobile operator receives a percentage of the business generated by the partner site.

Pricing models for mobile advertising include flat fee pricing, value-added pricing, cost per thousand impressions (CPM), and cost per click-throughs (CPC). In the flat fee pricing model, the mobile operator charges a fixed price for the advertisement for a given period. The value-added pricing model is a subcategory of flat fee pricing, in which the advertiser is charged with premium prices according to the time of the day or location of the target user. When the traffic information is available (such as number of visitors of a mobile portal or number messages sent), the mobile operator may charge the advertiser for every thousand people exposed to the advertisement. The CPM model provides a more reliable measure of advertisement effectiveness and thus presents a more rational way of pricing advertisements on the mobile medium. Such models provide more confidence on behalf of the advertising company. However, a more accountable way of charging for advertisements is applying the "cost per click-throughs" model. In this model, fees are based on actual click-throughs—in other words, how many customer responses were generated. Pricing based on the actual click-through rate guarantees that the user was not only exposed to the banner, but also decided to click on the banner and become exposed to the full-length target advertisement. Although CPC pricing is the most result oriented approach, it may not always be feasible for the mobile operator because only a relatively small proportion of banners are actually clicked on.

3

A Consumer-Centric Model for Successful Mobile Marketing

Overview of the M-Marketing Process

The most important prerequisite of any marketing effort is to place the consumer at the heart of planning, and mobile advertising is no exception. Any strategy is destined to fail if it does not adopt a consumer-centric perspective. Therefore, the purpose of this chapter is to present a consumer-centric model for a successful mobile marketing strategy that is based on the factors that influence consumers' intention to engage in and accept mobile marketing (Varnali, Yilmaz, and Toker, 2010).

The proposed strategy framework is a process model that starts with personalization and targeting. Once the consumer target segments are selected, the mobile marketer fine-tunes various features of the marketing message. Individual-based information, consumer history, cultural values, and device/channel characteristics are used as input for the personalization process which results in the creation of a highly customized mobile marketing message. When the message is ready, the next stage is to execute the mobile marketing campaign and communicate with the targeted users. At this stage the mobile marketer makes important strategic decisions such as message delivery time and location, the level of user control provided, and the level of viral marketing elements to be included. These message-related strategic decisions and other target, medium, and source related facilitators determine consumers' experience with mobile marketing. The third stage of the model focuses on consumers' perceptions, attitudes, and attention which collectively result in measurable behavioral outcomes.

The model, presented in Figure 3.1, is thought to be beneficial to both academics, by providing an integration of mobile consumer behavior research findings into a simple and coherent model of successful mobile marketing strategy, and to practitioners, by providing valuable inputs for setting up effective mobile marketing campaigns. The suggested conceptual model also provides insights into consumers' value creation process through mobile marketing and offers fruitful research avenues for marketing scholars.

Personalization/Targeting Process

Personalization is the degree to which a service/message is tailored to meet the needs and wants of the individual consumer. Personalization makes marketing messages increasingly relevant to the target consumer. Message relevance is one of the most important factors affecting consumer attitudes toward mobile advertising and is instrumental in minimizing the intrusiveness of the message. People who find mobile marketing campaigns

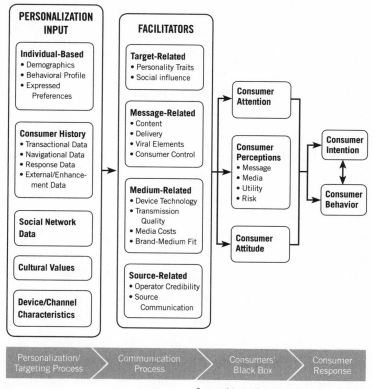

Source: Adapted from Varnali, Yilmaz, and Toker

FIGURE 3.1 A CONSUMER-CENTRIC MODEL FOR
MOBILE MARKETING

relevant are more likely to take action such as visiting a Web site, visiting a shop, replying to the message, providing personal information, engaging in word of mouth, or buying the product (Rettie, Grandcolas, and Deakins, 2005).

Personalization relies upon effective databases with sufficient active and potential customer entries and data-mining techniques. Such databases usually contain personal information about subscribers such as demographics (e.g., age, gender,

income, education, occupation, marital status), expressed preferences (e.g., favorite sports club, leisure activities, holidays, music
and media interests, community memberships, type of Internet
access), mobile device characteristics (e.g., brand, model, device
capabilities), and prior behavioral records (e.g., prior transactions, responses to marketing efforts, navigational data). For the
customer to provide this personal information, the mobile operator will have to offer an incentive, establish trust, and demonstrate credibility. In some instances, the advertiser's brand may
provide its own customer database, which may include other relevant information about target customers (e.g., product ownership information, prior transactional data). Personalization algorithms use all these data as inputs to create consumer segments
having distinct profiles. They then determine the type of information and services that will be delivered to the target customer
groups, the content and design of these marketing messages, and
their delivery terms (e.g., application type to be used, timing,
frequency). When the content and delivery of marketing messages are personalized to meet the needs and wants of different
customer groups, the likelihood of acceptance and the effectiveness of the message will be significantly increased.

Individual-Based Data

Different customers may perceive the value of an offering differ-
ently based on their personal values, needs, perceptions, interests,
and financial resources (Ravald and Grönroos, 1996). Therefore, personal characteristics and predispositions of mobile users
are important predictors of how mobile marketing practices
will be evaluated by different segments of consumers. Empiric

academic research found that demographics, personality traits, and cultural values do in fact influence perceptions about message/media/utility characteristics, which in turn influence attitudes toward and intention to engage in and accept mobile marketing practices.

There are two different types of individual-based data: explicit and implicit. Explicit data can be collected easily through various customer interfaces and by recording users' activities (e.g., knowledge, background, demographics, preferences, device characteristics, and prior behavioral records). Implicit data, on the other hand, are derived from explicit data by using conjunctive rules such as association and classification rules. Traditional targeting algorithms create user profiles based solely on explicit data. However, effective targeting should also utilize implicit data in order to create need-based (e.g., consumers with promotion versus socialization needs) and personality-trait–based (e.g., utilitarian versus hedonic tendencies) segmentation.

Demographics

Consumer demographics, such as gender, household income, age, education, social class, and student status are hard data and can be collected easily. A majority of the existing academic literature suggests that an individual's demographic profile has a significant influence on the adoption and usage of different mobile services and the acceptance of mobile marketing messages.

Age is a significant predictor of mobile service adoption and usage. Members of the younger generation, who grew up with mobile phones in their hands, have more confidence in the mobile technologies, and for them the mobile device is not only a source of communication, but it is also a source of entertainment and a tool for social expression. Young consumers show the most positive attitude toward various kinds of mobile services and are more willing to accept new services and content offered by the different mobile marketers. However, it is of value to note that young people use mobile phones primarily for socialization and convenient entertainment rather than for information and purchasing reasons, which are more appealing to more mature (older and more educated) users.

Gender, education, and income have also been found to influence consumers' attitude toward different types of mobile applications and moderate adoption and usage patterns. Normative pressure and intrinsic motives such as enjoyment are important determinants of the intention to use mobile services for female users, whereas extrinsic motives such as usefulness and expressiveness are the key drivers of mobile service usage and application preference for male users (Nysveen, Pedersen and Thorbjørnsen, 2005). Female users are more likely to visit the advertised shops via mobile marketing than male users are (Karjaluoto et al., 2008a). Socioeconomic status and maturity (measured by age and level of education) are also antecedents to consumers' value tendency, which influences consumers' service quality perceptions, which in turn predicts the level of satisfaction with the mobile service. Mobile users of lower maturity levels are more likely to have hedonic tendencies than those of a higher maturity level, who in contrast exhibit more utilitarian tendencies. Mobile users' hedonic tendency is found to be positively associated with perceptions of mobile Internet service quality. More importantly, the mobile users who have greater utilitarian tendencies are found to have more negative perceptions of mobile Internet service quality (Kim and Hwang, 2006).

Several other individual characteristics such as average volume of advertising messages received, prior nonstore shopping experience, prior usage of mobile services, and prior usage of the Internet are also influential in determining consumers' willingness to engage in and accept mobile marketing. Individuals who have no prior Internet experience differ considerably in terms of their attitude toward mobile advertising, entertainment, and shopping. It is worth noting that more experienced and more frequent users are more informed by interpersonal communication, while less experienced and nonusers are more informed by the mass media. Therefore, disseminating information regarding mobile services through the right mode of communication for different consumer segments is very important (Suoranta and Mattila, 2004).

Cultural Values

Culture is a complex and multifaceted construct which refers to the collection of relatively enduring and stable values that are shared among people in a specific society. Cultural values have long been recognized as a powerful force that shapes consumers' motivations, attitudes, and purchasing decisions. Various kinds of differences of consumer behavior patterns can be attributed to cultural differences (Hofstede, 1991).

Research on cross-cultures consistently shows that consumer behavior in individualist cultures is closely linked to attitudes, whereas behavior in collectivist cultures is closely linked to social norms (Bagozzi et al, 2000). Muk (2007) found empiric support for the aforementioned claim in the mobile context. His findings indicate that American consumers' decisions on accepting SMS ads are based solely on attitudinal considerations, whereas

Taiwanese consumers are influenced by both social norms and attitudinal factors. Since users in individualist societies rely more on their own experiences when forming their attitudes, "trialability" of mobile services, which refers to the extent to which potential adopters can try out mobile services, but decide to return to their prior conditions without great cost, should be more influential on their intention to adopt mobile services when compared to their counterparts in collectivist societies.

Another difference between individualist and collectivist cultures is the emphasis placed on privacy issues. Individualist societies are more concerned about privacy and thus perceive SMS advertising as more intrusive than their counterparts in collectivist cultures, who do not place such a high value on privacy.

As a result, understanding the orientation of cultural values in a specific market is an important prerequisite for successful mobile advertising. A generic mobile advertising campaign may not produce the same results in different cultural contexts. Therefore, personalization plans should take into account the cultural context in which the mobile advertising campaign will be run.

Consumer History

Consumer history refers to records of prior consumer behavior. It conveys "what the user does." It may include transactional data (e.g., prior mobile shopping experience, rate of refills, average return, prior downloads of mobile content, average volume of mobile ad messages received), navigational data (e.g., what kinds of WAP sites the user views, prior usage patterns of the mobile services, what kinds of banners does the user click), and response data (e.g., prior participation in instant-win campaigns, prior interaction with mobile marketing messages, prior responses to mobile offers, prior utilization of mobile discount coupons). It may also include external data (enhancement data) provided by third parties (e.g., advertiser brand, market research company, strategic partners). Such records of prior behavior of consumers are quite valuable because they reveal much about consumer preferences and possible future behavioral tendencies.

Recorded consumer history can be used to derive behavioral profiles of users and group them into segments with similar usage patterns, interests, and psychological traits. For example, an innovative personalization plan may use prior response data in order classify consumers according to their mental processing styles and create two segments of users as verbalizers and visualizers. Verbalizers will be those who are more responsive to text-based messages, whereas visualizers will be those who are more responsive to graphics-based messages. Such a segmentation method would be instrumental in message design. Visualizers will ignore long, complex, and unfamiliar texts; and verbalizers will find little value in visual content. Understanding such differences will aid marketers in tailoring messages for each group, which in turn would increase the effectiveness of mobile marketing campaigns.

Since each mobile device is typically used by one individual, mobile operators are able to build very rich customer databases with information that would be very difficult to collect via other media. The existence of such customer databases within the possession of mobile operators makes mobile marketing significantly superior to other marketing channels in terms of personalization and targeting ability.

Social Networks-Based Data

The essence of social communities rests on the principle that they are formed by individuals who share common goals, values, and interests. It is highly likely that an individual would be interested in "what" his peers are doing, "with whom" they are doing it, and "where" and "when" they are doing it. Such information would not only let the individual keep track of her social communities (hedonic motive), but it will also let her know about the latest offerings in the market that would appeal to her (utilitarian motive). Members of certain social networks tend to engage in the same activities, buy the same products and services, and behave similarly in particular situations. Therefore, mobile marketers can make accurate strategic predictions about the interests of a target user by collecting and evaluating information regarding attitudinal and behavioral characteristics of the other members of a specific social community.

This process is often called collaborative filtering. However, the algorithms of collaborative filtering have changed since their initial adoption by PC-based e-commerce sites. Traditionally, collaborative filtering meant recommending points of interest to users based on analyses of information from many transactions of many users. These algorithms identified offerings that suggest that if one is bought by a specific customer, that customer would also be interested in the other.

Today, collaborative filtering algorithms are much more powerful because of the depth and the amount of data available on the Internet. Apart from the rich customer data available to mobile network operators, they can identify community memberships through the up-to-date information available in mobile social networking sites, such as Twitter, Facebook, FriendFeed, and MySpace. These sites allow users to report any detailed action from their mobile phone to the whole community, which makes it visible to the marketers as well. Leave aside determining preferences, these platforms enable marketers to feed actual interests to users through the behaviors of other community members (e.g., six of your friends have bought this laptop, four of your friends have watched this movie, this activity is very popular among abc graduates, etc.).

Facilitators

There exists an array of facilitating factors that collectively determine the success of mobile marketing campaigns. These facilitating factors can be grouped under four main categories, namely target-related, source-related, message-related, and medium-related.

Target-Related Facilitators

Personality Traits

Personality traits of consumers usually moderate the relationship between success factors of mobile marketing and behavioral/attitudinal outcomes. Based on their deeply rooted personal traits, people may have divergent perceptions regarding the utility, emotional appeal, or relevance of the same mobile marketing message, the quality of the same mobile service, or the reliability of the mobile medium. The academic literature has identified a long list of relatively enduring and stable personal traits that may influence an individual's perceptions regarding a mobile marketing message and that individual's intention to accept and use mobile services. Personality traits can be considered as the ever-present lens through which an individual looks at the environment that surrounds him or her and interprets environmental stimuli. For example, time consciousness of a consumer moderates the relationships between convenience, user control, perceived risk, and cognitive effort with mobile channel value perceptions in such a way that for consumers with a high degree of time consciousness, the influence of time convenience and perceptions of user control on the creation of mobile service value will be stronger, whereas the influence of cognitive effort and perceived risk on mobile service value will be attenuated (Kleijnen, Ruyter, and Wetzels, 2007).

Mobile marketers should be aware of the significant influence of personality traits on service quality perceptions and consumer satisfaction, and they should find ways to fine-tune the application design, type, message content, frequency, and timing of message delivery on a one-to-one basis in order to achieve the expected results from mobile marketing efforts. The information provided in Table 3.1 should prove useful in effective personalization schemes.

TABLE 3-1   PERSONALITY TRAITS THAT MAY INFLUENCE PERCEPTION

Personality Trait	Definition
Innovativeness	The willingness of an individual to try out any new information technology
Opinion leadership	The extent to which a person is held in high esteem by those who accept his or her opinions
Concern for privacy	Anxiety or concern about various types of threats to the person's state of being free from intrusion
Optimum stimulation level	Individual's general responsiveness to environmental stimuli

Susceptibility to social influence	The degree to which one is being influenced by recommendations, actions, and adoption of products by significant others
Optimism	Overall positive feeling toward technological development
Attitude toward advertising	An individual's degree of like or dislike for advertising
Attitude toward the mobile medium	An individual's degree of like or dislike for the mobile medium
Critical mass	The minimal number of people who have already adopted the innovation necessary for adoption
Mobile technology readiness	An individual's propensity to use or embrace new technologies
Confidence in technology/Self-efficacy	Beliefs in one's capabilities to activate the motivation, cognitive resources, and courses of action needed to meet given situational demands
Love of shopping	The degree to which an individual receives emotional gratification from shopping
Time consciousness	Time awareness; time-conscious consumers are more prone to recognizing the scarcity of time as a resource
Personal attachment	The extent to which the mobile phone represents an integral part of a person's self-concept and defines his or her role in a cultural subgroup
Playfulness	Tendency to interact spontaneously, inventively, and imaginatively with microcomputers
Perceived financial resources	Individuals' subjective assessment of their economic resources and circumstances
Information-seeking behavior	Tendency to seek external information
Price consciousness	Customers who are interested in getting the lowest prices when they shop
Involvement level	The degree of intensity of interest that a buyer shows for a certain service in a specific purchase decision
Cultural background	Consumer's culture-based values, beliefs, and tendencies

Influence of Social/Peer Pressure

Social influence is an important determinant of intention and behavior. "People may choose to perform a behavior, even if they are not themselves favorable toward the behavior or its consequences, if they believe one or more important referents think they should, and they are sufficiently motivated to comply with the referents" (Venkatesh and Davis, 2000, p.187). People feel the need to obey social norms and therefore adopt behavioral patterns that comply with those of their desired social group. This way they strengthen their sense of belonging to the desired group, which helps them express their desired image in society at large. Using mobile services is no exception; indeed, many researchers have successfully validated extended versions of the theory of planned behavior (which suggests that subjective norms are significant drivers of intention to perform a behavior) in the mobile context. Further explanation for imitating peers' behavior is provided by social learning theory (Bandura, 1977), which emphasizes the relationship between information exchange and behavior change and stresses interpersonal links as the primary explanation of how individuals change their behavior. Collectively, these well-established theories suggest that managers must consider the social context in which mobile marketing is used.

Message-Related Facilitators

This section provides detailed information about the significance of the strategic decisions taken by the mobile marketer regarding the design and implementation of the mobile marketing stimuli (message). Message-related facilitators include design of the message content, time and place of delivery, the extent of consumer control provided, and optimization of the content for viral effect.

Influence of Message Content

The design of message content is the outcome of the personalization process. Personalization increases the relevance of the marketing message for the target consumer group, which in turn increases the effectiveness and acceptance of the marketing message. Rettie, Grandcolas, and Deakins (2005) found that people who find m-marketing campaigns relevant are more likely to take action such as visiting a Web site, visiting a shop, replying to a message, providing an e-mail address, or buying a product.

The fit between the message content and the personality characteristics and needs of the target consumer segment is an important predictor of success. Wording of the text, inclusion of graphical elements, the length of the message, inclusion and extensiveness of "how-to" directions, use of humor, how informative the message is, and inclusion of entertainment and socialization elements are all very important strategic message design issues that influence the acceptance and effectiveness of the marketing communication. Consumers with different personality traits and expertise levels will perceive different message designs as more appealing and enjoy different types of message content. So there is no global best way of designing a mobile marketing message. The most effective design depends on the target of the marketing message. Nevertheless, empiric studies suggest several rules of thumb such as the following:

- Be short and to the point
- Employ language understood by the target group
- Be entertaining for the target group
- Be attention grabbing

⦿ Be interesting and relevant to the target group (highly personalized)
⦿ Be actionable (interactive and calling to action)
⦿ Include incentives (instant win or lottery)
⦿ Include elements to facilitate viral effect (incentives for sharing, as little as advertising as possible, include self-expressive aspects)

Influence of Consumer Control

Explicit consumer permission is a significant predictor of the acceptance and success of mobile marketing practices. The target audience must be selected from subscribers who have opted-in to receive advertising from brands. Prior explicit permission is so critical that, without it, mobile marketing messages could reduce brand equity by causing resentment and irritation (Barwise and Strong, 2002). In all other marketing channels, consumers may simply choose to ignore or get away from a marketing effort if they are not interested in it or do not like it. However, when the marketing message is delivered to the mobile handset, it requires an action on behalf of the consumer (at worst the message must be deleted from the device), and the consumer is always notified about the delivery. Because of this very personal and "always-on" nature of mobile devices, the concept of intrusiveness is highly relevant in mobile marketing. Therefore, mobile advertising should be permission-based. If consumers have given their permission, they will be anticipating the marketing message (Godin, 1999), will feel as if they are in control of what is being sent to their mobile handsets, and hence will be less likely to take marketing as intrusive. In short, a successful mobile marketing campaign requires that consumers should have to opt in before they receive mobile advertising messages of any kind; have the ability to control timing, frequency, and content of the message; and have the option to opt out at any stage.

Influence of the Time and Location of Message Delivery

The timing of the mobile marketing message should be determined with the ultimate aim of delivering the message at the most appropriate time and location. In other words the mobile marketing communication should be contextually congruent both with the situation the user is in and the role the user is playing at that particular time (e.g., whether the user is managing a group of workers or nurturing a child). The delivery of customer service at the most appropriate time and location is the essence of contextual marketing, and mobile marketing is significantly superior to other media in capturing contextualization. Location sensing capability and the existence of effective customer databases enable mobile marketers to maximize the role and situation congruence of marketing communication for target individuals, and the mobile infrastructure permits marketers to deliver these messages with great precision, exactly at the time the message is intended to be delivered.

For example, in high-activity situations, mobile advertisements are perceived to be more intrusive than in situations with lower levels of activity (Wehmeyer, 2007). Similarly, entertainment-related messages may not be appreciated during working hours; discount coupons would be more effective if the promoted product or shop is nearby; and delivery of any kind of notification or update would be appreciated by the consumer when it is most needed, such as a reminder of a sports event delivered at a reasonable time before the event takes place or delivery of a financial update before the related markets are closed. Such contextualization can be captured only by the ubiquitous connection with customers that exists with mobile technology. The strategic mandate of contextual marketing is to be alongside the customer when and where he or she is in need of assistance or is ready to buy.

In the mobile Internet, contextual fit of the mobile banner is a crucial success factor for drawing attention and increasing the click-through rate. The click-through rates of WAP banners in WAP portals increase when they are placed under categories that are frequently viewed by their target consumer segment. Such placement not only enhances their targeting but also aids positioning strategies for those brands. For example, the banner of Nike Human Race is located under the category of fun, and the banner of Adidas is placed under the category of sports in the WAP portal of Turkcell.

Facilitating the Viral Effect

Mobile medium has a strong viral element. Mobile phones are becoming the primary means for communication among members of close social networks, especially for young people. Consumers may seek to participate in word-of-mouth—based promotions because they are consciously or unconsciously interested in being connected with a potential social network. It may be considered as a convenient way to remind others that he or she is an active member of that community. Therefore, people basically engage themselves in disseminating, receiving, or responding to socially relevant pieces of information in order to be a part of their peer community, and the most convenient way to engage in such activity is through the mobile medium because the mobile phone is ubiquitously connected to others.

Providing a viral element in a mobile advertising campaign would contribute significantly to its success. If the target population or the brand to be promoted is suitable for viral marketing, then the challenge is to design a mobile marketing message that should reach the maximum number of members of a target community via peer-to-peer messaging. Hence, the crucial question that should be asked prior to viral campaign design is, "What is most appreciated by peers of this community?" The starting point for investigation is the identification of common interests and the latest trends.

Moreover, since mobile phones are very intimate objects that are part of the personal spheres of individuals, personalization of them is a way of self-expression. People customize their handsets by downloading wallpapers, ringtones, and mobile applications. Peers have almost the same set of applications and mobile products downloaded to their handhelds, and they exchange various kinds of SMS/MMS messages.

In summary, including a viral element in a mobile marketing campaign, in other words designing and optimizing promotional messages to be passed on between consumers, would significantly increase message effectiveness. Viral mobile marketing could be based upon engaging and encouraging users to share messages, providing value in sharing a message, or making sharing messages inherent in participating in a particular campaign. The most prominent advantage of including a viral element in a campaign is that friend-to-friend referrals multiply the reach of the campaign exponentially which significantly increases the campaign's exposure at almost no additional cost.

Medium-Related Facilitators

Evidence suggests that attitudes toward mobile services improve as mobile devices and the underlying infrastructure improve in terms of usability, connection speed, quality, and reliability. Early versions of mobile devices had imposing constraints such as screen size, battery life, and limited processing power and memory. However, in recent years, with the improvements in microprocessor technologies, mobile devices have been transformed into smart-gadgets with larger high-resolution screens, tiny functional keypads, and increased memories. Now a number of mobile phone manufacturers offer true hybrid models that provide many of the features of PDAs and minicomputers. Handsets are also merging with other consumer electronics such as cameras, watches, and music players. The result is a market with a very broad range of devices with powerful technological features. Therefore, the technological capability of one's mobile device is an important facilitator of mobile marketing adoption. In order to increase the likelihood of compatibility, mobile marketers should deliver messages selectively to those handsets that can attractively display the marketing message and are capable of supporting the elicited consumer response.

The speed, quality, and reliability of the connection provided by the mobile operator are other significant facilitators of mobile marketing adoption. Traditionally, low transmission speeds and frequent disconnects limited mobile marketing adoption. Although, many operators now provide extended coverage areas and enhanced transmission speeds, disturbances and interruptions still occur because of congestion. Such instances create frustration and result in a negative attitude toward both the mobile service that is being used at that moment and the mobile operator providing the infrastructure. These problems will be lessened with the transition to third-generation telecommunication technologies which offer higher bandwidth and support higher data rates.

Brand-medium/application fit is another medium-related facilitator of campaign success. For example, SMS proved to be particularly successful in promoting frequently purchased low-budget items. SMS and MMS are useful for targeting younger users to announce events or support product launches. Also because of the personalized nature of many services, mobile advertising is more effective and suitable for promoting services rather than physical goods (Scharl, Dickinger, and Murphy, 2005). It should be noted that mobile marketing is much more comprehensive than mobile advertising. So the preceding arguments do not mean that mobile marketing is suitable only for the promotion of frequently purchased low-budget items and services. All kinds of brands and organizations can utilize the unique opportunities provided by different applications and tools of mobile marketing (e.g., SMS, MMS, WAP, IVR, CBC, mobile coupons, and games) in brand community building, customer relationship management, and viral marketing as well as in providing differentiated customer service. The challenge is to choose the appropriate mobile application type for different marketing purposes, brands, messages, and target customers.

The last medium-related facilitator is media cost. Although the competition among giant global mobile operators lowered prices from their highest levels, the cost for consumers to engage in mobile marketing practices remains relatively high. For example, GPRS and WAP charge the customer on the kilobyte of data transferred. When GPRS- or WAP-based applications are used for mobile marketing, there might be situations in which the air time can cause the users to exceed their prepaid minutes. Such situations may invoke frustration and resentment toward the mobile operator (Frolick and Chen, 2004). Mobile marketers should seek for ways to lower the perceived costliness of mobile marketing practices (e.g., offer discounts on monthly bills on the basis of acceptance of mobile advertising; provide incentives for participation).

Source-Related Facilitators

Consumer perceptions regarding various kinds of message source-related characteristics have the potential to influence effectiveness of the marketing communication. In mobile marketing, the receiver can attribute positive or negative feelings to both the actual source of the message (the sender of the message) and the operator who provides the medium for the message to be sent. Both source-related facilitators are equally important for the success of mobile communication.

First, let's elaborate on the impact of operator credibility and reputation on mobile marketing acceptance. Trust in the context of mobile marketing refers to a set of specific beliefs dealing primarily with the integrity, benevolence, competence, and predictability of a particular service provider. Trust elicits expectations of successful transactions and facilitates willingness to become vulnerable to a marketing effort after having taken its characteristics into consideration (Lee, 2005). Prior academic research provides empirical support for the positive influence of trust on attitudes toward mobile advertising and intentions to receive mobile messages (Karjaluoto et al., 2008b). In addition to its direct effects, trust also seems to make people feel more positive toward mobile marketing indirectly through increasing perceived usefulness of mobile ads (Zhang and Mao, 2008). So it is important for a mobile operator to improve its reliability and stability in order to provide its subscribers with positive experiences and increase their satisfaction and hence establish a trust-based reputation.

Because of the intimate nature of mobile devices, privacy issues are particularly sensitive with respect to mobile marketing. Besides worries about intrusion into one's private space, mobile spam raises privacy concerns related to the utilization of the personal and location information in the personalization of mobile marketing messages. Subscribers are likely to turn away from mobile service providers who are perceived as having inadequate safeguards in terms of privacy and security of their personal information. Operators must ensure their subscribers that wireless transactions are safe and that their personal information and privacy are being protected.

Second source-related facilitator constitutes the foundation of the viral effect. The actual source of the message (the identity of the message sender) may have a significant influence on the acceptance of mobile marketing messages. It has been found that people prefer to receive promotional messaging from another person rather than a company, would be more likely to perceive promotional messaging positively if it came from another person rather than if it came from a company, and the risk of brand damage is diminished if promotional messaging comes from another person within one's community instead of a company (Wais and Clemons, 2008).

The Consumers' Black Box

Perceptions and Attitudes

Users' intention to adopt and engage in mobile marketing practices is affected significantly by perceptions about the mobile marketing message, the application, and the medium itself. These perceptions predict consumers' attitude toward mobile marketing, which, together with social/peer pressure, are the most important direct drivers of willingness to engage in and accept mobile marketing. Therefore, knowledge regarding user perceptions of various dimensions of mobile marketing would provide valuable input for personalization plans in the process of designing effective mobile marketing messages and applications. This section elaborates on various perceptual characteristics that are identified as important predictors of mobile marketing acceptance.

User perceptions regarding the message content include perceived informativeness, entertainment, enjoyment, credibility, interactivity, simplicity, and usefulness. Informativeness and usefulness represent utilitarian benefits of a marketing message, whereas entertainment and enjoyment represent hedonic benefits. Although it is the value tendency of the individual or the purpose of usage that determines the relative importance of these benefits in influencing the consumer's intention to use mobile services, generally both have been found to have a significant impact on consumer attitudes. Users who engage in mobile marketing in pursuit of a specific outcome (e.g., participating for a monetary gain, making an urgent transaction, booking a ticket, looking for a destination) would value informativeness, usefulness, and simplicity more than its entertainment and enjoyment value.

The perceived credibility of the message content is related to trust toward the mobile marketer or toward the promoted brand. It is especially important in determining users' behavioral intention to click the wireless banner ads.

Perceived interactivity is related to the perceived quality of interaction and navigational ergonomics, which can be improved by designing easy-to-use, simple interaction interfaces, where relevant information is within immediate reach and navigation is easy to understand. Design aesthetics of the mobile interface is another important predictor of the perceived quality of the interaction. It refers to the balance, emotional appeal, or aesthetic of the user interface and may be expressed through colors, shapes, fonts, music, or animation.

User perceptions regarding the appropriateness of message delivery include perceived user control over frequency and timing and delivery of the message. If the user perceives that he or she is controlling what is being received, he or she would have a more positive attitude toward the marketing effort. Because of the personal nature of handheld mobile devices, mobile marketing campaigns should ultimately be permission-based. Sending unsolicited mobile messages is like committing brand suicide. It is worth noting that the frequency of mobile message sending is a sensitive issue. Although the number of messages should be high enough to remind customers about campaigns, a very high number of messages has a negative impact on perceived mobile advertising value, which ultimately causes negative perceptions about the brand and frustration with the mobile operator.

Application or service-specific user perceptions include perceived technical excellence (performance expectancy), ease of use (effort expectancy), cost and trialability. Perceived technical excellence refers to the degree to which the mobile service is perceived as being technically excellent in the process of providing promised benefits. Perceived ease of use refers to the degree to which a person believes that engaging with a mobile service would be free of effort. Performance expectancy and effort expectancy, together with perceived connection quality and reliability, determine the perceived convenience of the mobile service, which in turn has a strong impact on intention to engage in and accept it. In order to promote positive attitudes toward mobile marketing practices, marketers need to design mobile services that ubiquitously serve and support day-to-day individual and social practices which require very little prior experience and effort on behalf of the users.

Perceived trialability refers to the extent to which potential adopters can try out mobile applications; they can decide to return to their prior conditions without incurring great cost. Perceived trialability reinforces the adoption of new mobile services through reducing perceived risk and perceived cost.

Perceived risk is a major inhibitor of mobile marketing acceptance. It refers to the subjective expectation of suffering a loss in pursuit of the desired outcome of using a mobile service. It includes both monetary risks and privacy and security considerations. Security considerations refers to the security of the transaction, whereas privacy considerations refers to the extent to which users perceive having control over sharing personal information with others. Reducing perceived risk should be one of the most important issues in a mobile marketer's agenda. Several methods include strengthening the trust with the network operator via mass marketing and word-of-mouth marketing, establishing necessary technical protection measures against malicious third parties, and making these measures visible to subscribers, explicitly stating the commitment of the mobile marketer to protect customer privacy.

Perceptions regarding the mobile medium itself include perceived connection quality, perceived risk, and perceived expensiveness of the subscription. Perceived connection quality refers to the degree to which users perceive that the connection between the mobile device and the Internet is satisfying in terms of speed and reliability. Such perceptions are expected to improve significantly together with the widespread use of 3G networks.

Consumer Attention

Drawing consumers' attention is largely dependent on the content and context of the message. Therefore, effective personalization is the key to increasing attention, which in turn positions the offering into consumers' cognitive set of available alternatives to try. Attention is an important antecedent of consumer behavior, which sometimes may lead to impulsive trial of the offering. Although they are both components of the consumer's black box, consumer attitude toward a marketing offering is another strong determinant of attention, because, "Individuals with a persistent interest in a product class. . . are more likely to pay attention and to expend cognitive effort in processing the message of relevant advertisements" (Kokkinaki and Lunt, 1999, p. 49).

Consumer Response

Consumer behavior in general is defined as "the behavior that consumers display in searching for, purchasing, using, evaluating, and disposing of products and services that they expect will satisfy their needs" (Schiffman & Kanuk, 2007, p. 3). Consumer intention and consumer behavior (in terms of consumer response) represent the success measures of the conceptual model of mobile marketing success. The theory of planned behavior (Ajzen, 1985) suggests that there is a relationship between a consumer's attitude, the behavioral intention, and the observable behavior. Prior research in marketing has found repetitive evidence for these relationships that are actually bidirectional in nature. In the initial adoption process, the attitude toward an offering is an important determinant of consumer intention to try the offering. However, in the subsequent purchasing situations, satisfaction resulting from the prior experience is an important determinant of consumer intention and plays an important role in attitude formation. As a direct outcome of a customer's perception of value received, satisfaction is a strong predictor of repurchase intentions, complaining, product usage, word-of-mouth recommendations, and loyalty.

In any e-marketing campaign, especially in mobile marketing, the need to establish ways to identify visitors and their interaction is paramount. The personal nature of mobile handheld devices and the technological infrastructure that mobile marketing works on enable micromeasurement of advertising effectiveness. There are two kinds of metrics: exposure rate and interactivity data. Exposure rate reveals the reach of the advertisement and is usually measured by the number of times a visitor is exposed to the wireless ad. Although exposure measures are important in terms of measuring visibility of the ad and its reach, they do not measure effectiveness of the ad in terms of generating consumer response. Click-through rate is the most straightforward and accountable advertisement return rate measurement method that counts the number of visitors that actually click on a particular banner advertisement, or respond via SMS or IVR. SMS exposure is quite difficult to measure, because marketers can only statistically infer that a receiver actually read the SMS message instead of directly deleting it. Exposure and click-through measures are related to consumer awareness and attention, but they do not say much about consumers' like or dislike of the marketing communication or attitude change toward the marketed brand or service.

Interactivity data are compiled by logging the following information: how often a user visits a site, the number of repeat visits to the ad, where visitors tend to come from, how long they stay, the average number of pages they visit, most popular navigation patterns through the site, the most and least popular pages, and so on. Such data indicate the extent to which the mobile user actively engages with the mobile content. These measures provide information about consumer behavior patterns and hints about consumers' like or dislike for the ads, the mobile application, or the campaign as a whole. Repeat visits by the same user suggest a measure of loyalty.

Both exposure and interactivity metrics are important in assessing the effectiveness of the marketing campaign in terms of linking the advertisement with consumer outcomes. Exposure data measure consumers' awareness/attention, and interactivity data measure consumers' comprehension and like or dislike of the target ad. Mobile marketing campaigns are unique in terms of their ability to measure the real-time consumer response to a marketing stimulus due to the "always on" and "always with the user" characteristics of mobile handheld devices.

Some measurement terminology used in mobile marketing is provided here (Michael and Salter, 2006):

- ◉ *Visitor.* Individual who visits a wireless Web site or receives an SMS/MMS message.
- ◉ *Session.* A sequence of requests made by one user.
- ◉ *Ad/page views.* The number of times an ad is downloaded to a handheld device. If the same ad is located in multiple pages simultaneously, the number of views may be understated due to browser caching.
- ◉ *Click-through.* The number of times users click the mobile banner or respond to an SMS/MMS message.
- ◉ *Duration time.* Average time spent by a user on a single wireless Web page.
- ◉ *Gross impressions.* The gross sum of all exposures, which is measured by counting the number of unique visitors.
- ◉ *Reach.* The number of users that will be exposed to the mobile marketing campaign at least once in a given period.
- ◉ *Frequency.* The number of times a user is exposed to a particular advertising message.
- ◉ *Effective frequency.* The number of exposures necessary to stimulate recall or desired action.
- ◉ *Duplication.* The number of people who are exposed to a mobile ad in two or more situations.
- ◉ *Share.* The percentage of advertising impressions generated by all marketers in a category.
- ◉ *Composition.* The mixture of audience characteristics found in the audience for a campaign.
- ◉ *Page information transfers.* The true measurement of page deliveries to a handheld device and should be used when measuring the click-through rate. However, page information requests may not always represent actual figures because of incomplete information transfers.

4

The Future of
Mobile Marketing

Future Prospects

Different countries and regions exist in the different eras of mobile marketing simultaneously, hence the expression "future of mobile marketing" does not imply the same meaning for everyone globally. Many mobile applications that will be offered as novelties in some markets are already in use in some others, such as mobile TV, video streaming, and applications that require broadband connection speeds. Nevertheless, globally speaking, mobile marketing revenues are increasing at a rapid pace, and most of the mobile marketing practices have not even reached their full potential yet. A report by Dentsu (2009) states that mobile advertising revenue per user in Japan has increased from $1 per year in 2003 to $11 per year in 2009. Coda Research Consultancy (2010) estimates that mobile broadband search and display ad revenues in the United States will grow to $4.2 billion in 2015, up from $1 billion in 2010. It is predicted that nearly 70 percent of those revenues will come from search advertising. In another report by Juniper Research (2009), the mobile entertainment market is expected to grow at an average annual rate of 15.2 percent over the next five years. It expects music downloads to be the most successful element in the mobile entertainment services in terms of revenue generation, followed by mobile games. SMS revenues are projected to decline in the next five years, but the increase in mobile advertising revenue from search and display will compensate for it and make the segment grow faster than regular Internet advertising. Although these forecasts can be positively or negatively affected by economic developments, the figures demonstrate a huge business potential for the mobile industry.

Over the course of the past few years, use of mobile Internet evolved from an occasional activity to become a daily part of people's lives. This highlights the mounting importance of the mobile medium as consumers become more reliant on their mobile handsets to access time-sensitive and utilitarian information. According to *Mobile Marketing Magazine* (2009), in the United States the fastest-growing categories accessed via the mobile Web are social networking sites or blogs, which grew by 427 percent between January 2008 and January 2009; trading and financial account sites, which grew by 188 percent; and movie information, which grew by 185 percent. It should be noted that much of the growth in mobile Internet usage is driven by the increased popularity of downloaded applications, such as those offered for iPhone and BlackBerry. It is predicted that more people will access the Internet from their mobile than their PC in the future. According to T-Mobile Germany, there was 30 times more browsing on iPhones than on other handsets, and at Vodafone Germany, 45 percent of data ARPU (average revenue per user) already are attributable to the mobile Internet, due to partnerships with Google, YouTube, and MySpace, and use of widgets.

In recent years, there have been significant changes in the mobile environment. In addition to the global financial crisis, the regulatory and competitive pressures the operators face are escalating. Profit margins from mature voice markets are falling, and customer demand for converged and differentiated services as well as devices is mounting. Therefore, in order to sustain operating margins, operators must become more efficient in delivery of services and enrich their range of services with a consumer-centric approach. The shares of value-added services and mobile advertising in global revenues of mobile operators continue to grow steadily. This highlights the importance of innovativeness and creativity in the design of new mobile applications and services that have the potential to create value for both mobile users and for the partners of the mobile value chain. In the process, mobile network operators need to transform themselves from traditional mobile voice carriers to mobile service providers in order to maintain their position at the center of the mobile value chain and to be able to capture a more lucrative portion of the revenues generated through the mobile medium.

Together with the launch and widespread adoption of 3G technology, the mobile marketing department of Turkcell expects the following developments:

⊙   With Internet services gravitating toward mobile Internet, new business models such as advertising-based services will, as a result, become the order of the day. The mobile environment will increasingly become a more attractive marketing medium, and more multichannel marketing efforts will include mobile marketing practices.

- The mobile medium will make it possible to extend health services to remote areas. Several health-related applications are already in use. It is expected that these types of applications will improve significantly and hence their adoption will increase.

- Mobile applications that allow doctors to diagnose and follow up on patients remotely will be more effective and common. (Examples exist in Africa, South America, and Southeast Asia.) For instance, patients will be able to show their X-rays and laboratory test results to a doctor without having to go to a hospital.

- Distance learning will become more prevalent. Equal opportunity in education will be provided with distance learning applications.

- With the help of the mobile medium, emergency action and control will be much easier in times of disaster.

- New business models will evolve between the state and the private sectors.

- Providing public services via the mobile medium will be more prevalent (e.g., m-health, m-learning, m-government).

- The share of mobile commerce in total e-commerce will continue to grow.

- It will be more common to be able to shop without having to carry a wallet.

⦿ As the penetration rate of 3G-enabled smartphones increases, the concept of the mobile office (that allows people to access their files at the office at a very high speed using mobile handsets) will be more common.

⦿ Smart home applications will be more common (e.g., the ability to operate home appliances with a mobile device before coming home).

⦿ Mobile applications that converge the real world with the digital world (such as location-aware mobile social networking applications, mobile tagging based applications, mobile applications that provide augmented reality) have already started to change interaction and communication patterns both among consumers and between consumers and brands. Widespread adoption of these applications will also change the nature of the information available on the Internet. Increased rate of updates will reveal real-time information about the users, and hence the value of a chunk of information will decay much faster.

⦿ The value of mobile advergaming (mobile games sponsored by brands that include embedded advertising messages) will be appreciated more by brands, which will expand the market for mobile entertainment. In addition to mobile advergaming, fueled with faster data rates, a variety of content services (e.g., MobileTV, VOD content, mobile music, virtual magazines) will proliferate, which would expand the market for mobile marketing.

Although 3G infrastructure has not been launched to its full extent in many regions, or its promises have not yet been fully acknowledged in those countries where it has already been launched, researchers and industry pioneers have already been expressing a growing interest in 4G wireless networks. The future of mobile, 4G, is not only about enhanced data rates. Its essence is about convergence and enhanced coverage. 4G wireless networks will support seamless roaming across multiple wireless technologies. Subscribers' connections will be automatically handled by different access technologies surrounding users (e.g., LAN, Wi-Fi, cellular networks, satellite-based networks) according to users' predefined preferences such as cost minimization or data rate maximization. With this feature, users will have access to divergent services, increased coverage, the convenience of a single device, one bill with reduced total access cost, and more reliable wireless access even in cases of failure or loss of one or more networks. Although several mobile devices have already started to provide users with the option of choosing from among different access types for data transmission (e.g., Wi-Fi or GPRS), the complete employment of 4G environment requires several major issues to be resolved, such as intersystem operability, automatic handover procedures, and billing and pricing (Kastro, 2004). Despite technological challenges ahead, 4G networks will eventually be deployed and will provide mobile marketers with new and exciting features that are envisioned to aid in the enhancement of the mobile customer experience.

Concluding Remarks

Less than 10 years ago mobile phones were handy gadgets of interpersonal communication with so many technological limitations that they were only capable of playing monotones, entertaining the user with simple puzzle games, and keeping a short list of phone numbers in their memory. Today they are capable of storing gigabytes of data, function as multi-megapixel digital cameras, music players, and little smart PCs that allow users to surf the Internet, share user-generated content with friends, play multiplayer games, and even watch TV. The penetration rates are over 100 percent in many of the developed countries and continue to rise steadily all around the world. Mobile advertising revenues are growing, and mobile services are becoming indispensible for many users.

Mobile marketing made a humble start, but its future is bright. Seeing the opportunity, firms have started to allocate more and more budget for mobile marketing, which has made the mobile marketing value chain flourish. This book provides an overall picture of the mobile marketing phenomenon in order to act as a handbook for starters in the mobile marketing business. We present a comprehensive definition of the concept of mobile marketing, elaborate on a variety of mobile marketing tools and applications, discuss medium-specific challenges and benefits for marketers, and suggest a consumer-centric model of successful mobile marketing. Throughout the course of the book various real market examples are provided to illustrate the concepts that are being discussed. We hope the book has provided answers to many of your questions.

The Turkish GSM Market

There exist three mobile operators in Turkey: Turkcell, Vodafone, and Avea. As of June 2010, there were 61.5 million mobile subscribers in Turkey, which is approximately 84 percent penetration rate. The Turkish population is young with an estimated average age of 29, which is lower than elsewhere in western Europe, and the majority of the population lives in urban areas. These factors suggest further growth potential for the mobile communications market in Turkey.

GSM-based mobile communication started in Turkey when Turkcell began its operations in February 1994. Turkcell and Telsim were granted a 25-year GSM license upon payment of an up-front license fee of $500 million each. Telsim was seized by the Savings Deposit Insurance Fund (SDIF) in February 2004, and it was put up for sale by the SDIF in August 2005. An auction was held for Telsim on December 13, 2005, with Vodafone submitting the winning bid of $4.55 billion. The sale process was completed on May 24, 2006. In 2000, two new GSM 1800

The source for this Appendix is http://www.turkcell.com.tr.

licenses were issued. One of the licenses was awarded to Is-Tim, a company that began offering GSM services in March 2001 under the Aria brand name. The company was formed by Telecom Italia Mobile and Isbank, one of the largest private banks in Turkey. Is-Tim paid a license fee of $2.5 billion excluding taxes. The other GSM 1800 license was awarded to Turk Telekom. Turk Telekom began offering GSM services on December 14, 2001, through its brand Aycell. In February 2004, Is-Tim and Aycell merged to form TT&TIM, which is owned by Turk Telekom (40 percent), Telekom Italia Mobile (40 percent), and Isbank (20 percent). TT&TIM operated under the brand name of Avea. Market shares of these three mobile operators are shown in Figure A.1.

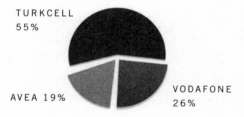

TURKCELL 55%

AVEA 19%

VODAFONE 26%

FIGURE A.1 MARKET SHARES OF MOBILE OPERATORS IN TURKEY AS OF JUNE 2010

Regulation of the Turkish Telecommunications Industry

All telecommunications activity in Turkey is regulated by the Ministry of Transportation and the Information Technologies and Communications Authority. The Telegram and Telephone Law No. 406 (the telecommunications law), as amended, is the principal law governing telecommunications activity in Turkey. The wireless law No. 2813, as amended, and Ministry of Transportation Law No. 3348, as amended, also include provisions relating to telecommunications in Turkey.

The telecommunications law was reformed in 2000 and 2001. The reforms were aimed at modernizing and reforming the legal and institutional framework for the provision of telecommunications infrastructure and service in Turkey.

The Information Technologies and Communications Authority is an independent telecommunications regulator with financial and administrative independence. It has the authority to grant licenses and set fees in the telecommunications sector.

For further information regarding the Information Technologies and Communications Authority, contact http://www.btk.gov.tr/Eng/english.htm

Additional Cases

The information regarding the real-market mobile marketing cases that follow is provided by the Mobile Marketing Department of Turkcell.

No part of the material provided in this section may be reproduced without the written permission of Turkcell.

Case 1: Renault—MMS

Challenge. To promote and increase brand exposure of Renault Symbol just before the Auto Show, Istanbul.

Method. Auto Show tickets were used as an incentive to encourage targeted users to engage in an MMS quiz about Renault Symbol.

Targeting criteria:
- Male
- Age: 25+
- Billing address: Istanbul
- Been in Istanbul in the last month
- Owns a car
- Participates in fuel oil campaigns

- Attended Formula 1 in 2007
- Attended CNR Auto Show in 2007
- Sends/receives five MMS per month
- Heavy user of SMS

Results. Return rate: 5 percent. All tickets were given out within the first 20 minutes.

Translation: Have you met with NEW SYMBOL? Type NEW SYMBOL and send it to 3141. Be among the first 20 to answer the questions. Win a ticket to AUTOSHOW and meet with NEW SYMBOL.

Case 2: Denizbank—SMS

Challenge. To facilitate personal credit applications via SMS.

Method. Users were informed that Denizbank accepted personal credit applications via SMS (that included user's national identity number) and to respond within five minutes. No further questions were asked.

Targeting criteria:

- Male
- Age: 30+
- Living in Istanbul, Ankara, Izmir
- SMS outgoing segment: 30+

Denizbank'tan evraksiz kefilsiz cebimde kredi. KREDiM yaz bosluk birak T.C. KiMLiK NUMARANI yaz 3280'e gonder kredi cevabin 5 dakikada cebine gelsin.

Translation: Denizbank offers loans with no guarantor or application forms. Text CREDIT, leave a blank, and text YOUR PERSONAL ID to 3280; your credit response will be sent to your cell phone.

- SMS incoming segment: 5–60
- Uses SMS services of other banks

Results. Return rate: 10 percent

Case 3: NARCITY—SMS

Challenge. To facilitate sales of residences in Narcity, Istanbul, a housing project of Tepe Insaat Co, and advertise the sample model apartment.

Method. Target customers were informed of the 20 percent discount in advance and were directed to contact the center via SMS.

Targeting criteria:

- Female:
  - Age: 25–50
  - Living in Istanbul
  - Prior participation in shopping campaigns
  - A–B segment
  - Message text included emphasis on Laura Ashley designs
- Male:
  - Age: 20–60
  - Living in Istanbul
  - Car owner
  - Roaming in the last three months
  - A–B segment

> Tepe Insaat Narcity'de simdi peşin alana 4+1'ler %20'ye varan indirimle! Laura Ashley dekorasyonlu 4+1 örnek dairemizi mutlaka görün!
> 02164444627

Translation: Tepe Insaat Narcity offers 4+1 flats with 20% off in cash payments. Please see the show flat decorated by Laura Ashley! 02164444627

Results. Return rate: 16 percent.
20 residences were sold after message delivery.

Case 4: P&G—IVR

Challenge. To facilitate participation in an FMCG promotion campaign and strengthen brand image.

Method. Target customers were informed of the existing campaign via IVR. Additionally, users who pressed 1 received an SMS including brief details about the campaign.

Targeting criteria:
- Female
- Age: 25–40
- Living in targeted cities
- Participated in FMCG campaigns at least three times in the last three months

Results. 70 percent of respondents listened to the campaign sound clip until the end. Sales increased in those cities in which the IVR campaign was launched. P&G Global rated the campaign as best practice.

Case 5: Austrian Airlines— SMS and WAP Push

Challenge. To obtain permission from customers in order to send promotional mobile ads regarding campaigns for Austrian Airlines.

Method. Target consumers were informed about the RedTicket campaign of Austrian Airlines via SMS. The text message included a WAP push link and also asked users to provide permission for future mobile ad delivery by sending an SMS to 3455.

Targeting criteria:

- Traveled abroad at least two times in the last six months
- Age: 25–50
- Living in Istanbul, Izmir, Ankara
- A–B–C1 segments
- SMS outgoing segment: 15+
- Sensitive to promotions

Results. Return rate: 11 percent

Avusturya Havayollari ile REDTICKET.
98€'dan baslayan fiyatlarla Avrupa.
www.austrian.com
REDTICKET avantajlari icin KAYIT
yazip 3455'e sms gonderiniz.

Translation: Austrian Airlines and REDTICKET. Fly to Europe starting from 98£. www.austrian.com. For further REDTICKET advantages text KAYIT to 3455.

Case 6: Société Générale—SMS

Challenge. To facilitate personal credit applications via SMS.

Method. Users were informed that the bank would accept personal credit applications up to 30,000 TL via SMS (that included user's national identity number). The SMS included information about the attractive interest rate and extended due date.

Targeting criteria:

- Male
- Age: 25–50
- Monthly bill < 100 TL
- Living in Istanbul, Izmir, Ankara
- SMS outgoing segment: 30+
- SMS incoming segment: 5–60
- Subscription length: at least six months
- Not a member of Kampuscell (the billing tariff for university students)

Results. 20 percent of respondents have applied for a personal loan.

References

Ajzen, I. (1985) From Intentions to Actions: A Theory of Planned Behavior. In J. Kuhl and J. Beckmann (eds.), *Action Control: From Cognition to Behavior.* New York: Springer-Verlag.

Anckar, B., and D'Incau, D. (2002) Value creation in mobile commerce: findings from a consumer survey. *JITTA: Journal of Information Technology Theory and Application,* 4(1), 43–65.

Bagozzi, R., Wong, N., Abe, S., and Bergami, M. (2000) Cultural and situational contingencies and the theory of reasoned action: application to fast food restaurant consumption. *Journal of Consumer Psychology,* 9(2), 97–106.

Bandura, A. (1977) *Social Learning Theory.* New York: General Learning Press.

Barnes, S. J. (2003) Location-based services: the state of the art. *e-Service Journal,* 2(3), 59–71.

Barwise, P., and Strong, C. (2002) Permission-based mobile advertising. *Journal of Interactive Marketing,* 16(1), 14–24.

Berthon, P., Pitt, L. F. and Watson, R. T. (2000) Postmodernism and the Web: meta themes and discourse. *Technological Forecasting and Social Change,* 65(3), 265–279.

Capon, N., and Glazer, R. (1987) Marketing and technology: a strategic coallignment. *Jounal of Marketing*, 51 (July), 1–14.

Carroll, A., Barnes, S. J., Scornavacca, E., and Fletcher, K. (2007) Consumer perceptions and attitudes towards SMS advertising: recent evidence from New Zealand. *International Journal of Advertising*, 26(1), 79–98.

Childers, T. L., Carr, C. L., Peck, J., and Carson, S (2001) Hedonic and utilitarian motivations for online retail shopping behavior. *Journal of Retailing*, 77, 511–535.

Clarke, I. (2001) Emerging value propositions for m-commerce. *Journal of Business Strategies*, 18(2), 133–149.

Coda Research Consultancy (2010) US mobile advertising revenues with forecasts to 2015.

Davis, F. D. (1989) Perceived usefulness, perceived ease of use, and user acceptance of information technology. *MIS Quarterly*, 13(3), 318–341.

Fishbein, M., and Ajzen, I. (1975) *Beliefs, Attitude, Intention and Behavior: An Introduction to Theory and Research*. MA: Addison-Wesley.

Frolick, M. N., and Chen, L. (2004) Assessing m-commerce opportunities. *Information Systems Management*, 21(2), 53–62.

Germanakos, P., Tsianos, N., Lekkas, Z., Mourlas, C., and Samaras, G. (2008) Improving m-commerce services effectiveness with the use of user-centric content delivery. *Journal of Electronic Commerce in Organizations*, 6(1), 1–19.

Godin, S. (1999) *Permission Marketing: Turning Strangers into Friends, and Friends into Customers*. New York: Simon & Schuster.

Hofstede, G. (1991) *Cultures and Organizations: Software of the Mind*. London: McGraw-Hill.

Juniper Research (2008a) Mobile Advertising Strategies and Forecasts.

Juniper Research (2008b) Mobile Ticketing and Coupons: Strategies & Markets.

Juniper Research (2009) Mobilising Entertainment in the Downturn.

Kaasinen, E. (2003) User needs for location-aware mobile services. *Personal and Ubiquitous Computing*, 7(1), 70–79.

Karjaluoto, H., Lehto, H., Leppäniemi, M., and Jayawardhena, C. (2008a) Exploring gender influence on customer's intention to engage permission-based mobile marketing. *Electronic Markets*, 18(3), 242.

Karjaluoto, H., Standing, C., Becker, M., and Leppaniemi, M. (2008b) Factors affecting Finnish consumers' intention to receive SMS marketing: a conceptual model and an empirical study. *International Journal of Electronic Business*, 6(3), 298–318.

Kastro, Y. (2004) Migration and integration strategies towards 4G networks. *Boaziçi University Department of Computer Engineering*, unpublished article.

Kim, D. J., and Hwang, Y. (2006) A Study of Mobile Internet Usage from Utilitarian and Hedonic User Tendency Perspectives. *Proceedings of the Twelfth Americas Conference on Information Systems*.

Kim, H., Chan, H. C., and Gupta, S. (2007) Value-based adoption of mobile Internet: An empirical investigation. *Decision Support Systems*, 43(1), 111–126.

Kleijnen, M., Ruyter, K., and Wetzels, M. (2007) An assessment of value creation in mobile service delivery and the moderating role of time consciousness. *Journal of Retailing*, 83(1), 33–46.

Kokkinaki, F., and Lunt, P. (1999) The effect of advertising message involvement on brand attitude accessibility. *Journal of Economic Psychology*, 20(1), 41–51.

Krishnamurthy, S. (2001) A comprehensive analysis of permission marketing. *Journal of Computer Mediated Communication*, 6(2).

Lee, T. (2005) The impact of perceptions of interactivity on customer trust and transaction intentions in mobile commerce. *Journal of Electronic Commerce Research*, 6(3), 165–181.

Li, H. S., Edwards M., and Lee J. (2002) Measuring the intrusiveness of advertisements: Scale development and validation. *Journal of Advertising*, 31(2), 37–47.

Mahatanankoon, P. (2007) The effects of personality traits and optimum stimulation level on text-messaging activities and m-commerce intention. *International Journal of Electronic Commerce*, 12(1), 7–30.

Mahatanankoon, P., Wen, H. J., and Lim, B. (2005) Consumer-based m-commerce: Exploring consumer perception of mobile applications. *Computer Standards & Interfaces*, 27(4), 347–357.

Michael, A., and Salter, B. (2006) *Mobile Marketing: Achieving Competitive Advantage through Wireless Technology*. UK: Butterworth-Heinemann.

Mobile Marketing Association (2009) *Mobile Marketing Industry Glossary*. http://mmaglobal.com/glossary.pdf.

Mobile Marketing Magazine (2008) *The Future of Mobile*,

According to Airwide. http://www.mobilemarketingmagazine
.co.uk (December 11, 2008).

Mobile Marketing Magazine (2009) *US Mobile Web Use Doubles in a Year.* http://www.mobilemarketingmagazine.co.uk (March 19, 2009).

Mort, G. S., and Drennan, J. (2002) Mobile digital technology: Emerging issues for marketing. *Journal of Database Marketing*, 10(1), 9–24.

Muk, A. (2007) Cultural influences on adoption of SMS advertising: a study of American and Taiwanese consumers. *Journal of Targeting, Measurement and Analysis for Marketing*, 16, 39–47.

Nysveen, H., Pedersen, P. E., and Thorbjørnsen, H. (2005) Intentions to use mobile services: antecedents and cross-service comparisons. *Journal of the Academy of Marketing Science*, 33(3), 330–347.

Ondrus, J., and Pigneur, Y. (2006) Towards a holistic analysis of mobile payments: a multiple perspectives approach. *Electronic Commerce Research and Applications*, 5(3), 246–257.

Pedersen, P. E., Methlie, L. B., and Thorbjørnsen, H. (2002) Understanding Mobile Commerce End-User Adoption: A Triangulation Perspective and Suggestion for an Exploratory Service Evaluation Framework. *Proceedings of the 35th Hawaii International Conference on System Sciences.*

Ravald, A., and Grönroos, C. (1996) The value concept and relationship marketing. *European Journal of Marketing* 30(2), 19–30.

Rettie, R., Grandcolas, U., and Deakins, B. (2005) Text message advertising: response rates and branding effects.

Journal of Targeting, Measurement and Analysis for Market-ing, 13(4), 304–313.

Rogers, E. M. (1983) *The Diffusion of Innovation*. New York: Free Press.

Salo, J., and Karjaluoto, H. (2007) Mobile games as an advertising medium: towards a new research agenda. *Innovative Marketing*, 3(1), 71–84.

Scharl, A., Dickinger, A., and Murphy, C. (2005) Diffusion and success factors of mobile marketing. *Electronic Commerce Research and Applications*, 4, 159–173.

Sood, A., and Tellis, G. J. (2005) Technological evolution and radical innovation. *Journal of Marketing*, 69(3), 152–168.

Suoranta, M., and Mattila, M. (2004) Mobile banking and consumer behaviour: new insights into the diffusion pattern. *Journal of Financial Services Marketing*, 8(4), 354N366.

Turkish Statistical Institute (2008) *Communication Statistics*. http://www.turkstat.gov.tr/VeriBilgi.do?tb_id=54&ust_id=15.

Turkish Statistical Institute (2008) *ICT Usage Statistics*. http://www.turkstat.gov.tr/PreTablo.do?tb_id=60&ust_id=2.

Varnali, K., Yilmaz, C., and Toker, A. (2010) Drivers of Success in Mobile Marketing. *Bogazici University Working Paper*.

Venkatesh, V., and Davis, F. D. (2000) A theoretical extension of the technology acceptance model: four longitudinal field studies. *Management Science*, 46(2), 186–204.

Wais, J. S., and Clemons, E. K. (2008) Understanding and implementing mobile social advertising. *International Journal of Mobile Marketing*, 3(1), 12–18.

Wehmeyer, K. (2007) Mobile Ad Intrusiveness–The Effects of

Message Type and Situation. *Proceedings of the 20th Bled eConference.*

Wu, J., and Wang, S. (2005) What drives mobile commerce? An empirical evaluation of the revised technology acceptance model. *Information & Management*, 42(5), 719–729.

Zhang, J., and Mao, E. (2008) Understanding the acceptance of mobile SMS advertising among young Chinese consumers. *Psychology & Marketing*, 25(8), 787–805.

Other Related Scholarly Sources

Aungst, S. G., and Wilson, D. T. (2005) A primer for navigating the shoals of applying wireless technology to marketing problems. *The Journal of Business & Industrial Marketing*, 20(2/3), 59–70.

Balasubramanian, S., Peterson, R. A., and Jarvenpaa, S.L. (2002) Exploring the implications of m-commerce for markets and marketing. *Journal of the Academy of Marketing Science*, 30(4), 348–361.

Barnes, S. J. (2002) The mobile commerce value chain: analysis and future developments. *International Journal of Information Management*, 22(2), 91–108.

Barnes, S. J. (2002) Provision of services via the wireless application protocol: A strategic perspective. *Electronic Markets*, 12(1), 14–21.

Barnes, S. J., and Scornavacca, E. (2004) Mobile marketing: the role of permission and acceptance. *International Journal of Mobile Communications*, 2(2), 128–139.

Barutçu, S. (2007) Attitudes towards mobile marketing tools: a study of Turkish consumers. *Journal of Targeting, Measurement and Analysis for Marketing*, 16, 26–38.

Bauer, H. H., Reichardt, T., Barnes S. J., and Neumann, M. M. (2005) Driving consumer acceptance of mobile marketing: a theoretical framework and empirical study. *Journal of Electronic Commerce Research*, 6(3), 181–192.

Bauer, H. H., Reichardt, T., Exler, S., and Tranka, E. (2007) Utility-based design of mobile ticketing applications— a conjoint-analytical approach. *International Journal of Mobile Communications*, 5(4), 457–473.

Bayartsaikhan, K., Danielak, P., Dunst, K., Guibert, J., Luxford, L., Romanossian, R., Storti, M., and Seal, K. C. (2007) Market for third screen: a study of market potential of mobile TV and video across the U.S. and selected European countries. *International Journal of Mobile Marketing*, 2(1), 12–27.

Becker, D. (2007) Participation TV: premium SMS vs. toll-free IVR. *International Journal of Mobile Marketing*, 2(2), 50–52.

Bertelè, U., Rangone, A., and Renga, F. (2002) Mobile Internet: an empirical study of B2C WAP applications in Italy. *Electronic Markets*, 12(1), 27–37.

Bhatti, T. (2007) Exploring factors influencing the adoption of mobile commerce. *Journal of Internet Banking and Commerce*, 12(3), 2–13.

Bigne, E., Ruiz, C., and Sanz, S. (2005) The Impact of Internet user shopping patterns and demographics on consumer mobile buying behaviour. *Journal of Electronic Commerce Research*, 6(3), 193–210.

Bigné, E., Ruiz, C., and Sanz S. (2007) Key Drivers of Mobile Commerce Adoption: An Exploratory Study of Spanish Mobile Users. *Journal of Theoretical and Applied Electronic Commerce Research*, 2(2), 48-61.

Bruner, G. C., and Kumar, A. (2005) Explaining consumer acceptance of handheld Internet devices. *Journal of Business Research*, 58(5), 553–558.

Chae, M., Kim, J., Kim, H., and Ryu, H. (2002) information quality for mobile Internet services: a theoretical model with empirical validation. *Electronic Markets*, 12(1), 38–46.

Chen, J. V., Ross, W., and Huang, S. F. (2008) Privacy, trust, and justice considerations for location-based mobile telecommunication services. *The Journal of Policy, Regulation and Strategy for Telecommunications, Information and Media*, 10(4), 30.

Chen, L. (2008) A model of consumer acceptance of mobile payment. *International Journal of Mobile Communications*, 6(1), 32–52.

Choi, J., Seol, H., Lee, S., Cho, H., and Park, Y. (2008) Customer satisfaction factors of mobile commerce in Korea. *Internet Research*, 18(3), 313–335.

Chowdhury, H. K., Parvin, N., Weitenberner, C., and Becker, M. (2006) Consumer attitude toward mobile advertising in an emerging market: an empirical study. *International Journal of Mobile Marketing*, 1(2), 33–42.

Coursaris, C., Hassanein, K., and Head, M. (2003) M-commerce in Canada: an interaction framework for wireless privacy. *Canadian Journal of Administrative Sciences*, 20(1), 54–74.

Cyr, D., Head, M., and Ivanov, A. (2006) Design aesthetics leading to m-loyalty in mobile commerce. *Information & Management*, 43, 950–963.

DeBaillon, L., and Rockwell, P. (2005) Gender and student-status differences in cellular telephone use. *International Journal of Mobile Communications*, 3(1), 82–98.

Denk, M., and Hackl, M. (2004) Where does mobile business go? *International Journal of Electronic Business*, 2(5), 480.

Dholakia, R. R., and Dholakia, N. (2004) Mobility and markets: emerging outlines of m-commerce. *Journal of Business Research*, 57, 1391–1396.

Dolian, B. (2008) Text-to-screen emerges: a conceptual approach to a powerful interactive marketing tool. *International Journal of Mobile Marketing*, 3(1), 81–85.

Doolin, B., and Ali, E. A. H. (2008) Adoption of mobile technology in the supply chain: an exploratory cross-case analysis. *International Journal of E-Business Research*, 4(4), 1–16.

Gao, Q., Rau, P. P., and Salvendy, G. (2010) Measuring perceived interactivity of mobile advertisements. *Behaviour & Information Technology*, 29(1), 35–44.

Gressgard, L. J., and Stensaker, I. (2006) The mobile service industry: strategic challenges and future business models. *International Journal of Mobile Communications*, 4(5), 509–531.

Haaker, T., Faber, E., and Bouwman, H. (2006) Balancing customer and network value in business models for mobile services. *International Journal of Mobile Communications*, 4(6), 645–661.

Haghirian, P., and Inoue, A. (2007) An advanced model of consumer attitudes toward advertising on the mobile internet. *International Journal of Mobile Communications*, 5(1), 48–67.

Hairong L., and Stoller, B. (2007) Parameters of mobile advertising: a field experiment. *International Journal of Mobile Marketing*, 2(1), 4–11.

Hanley, M., Becker, M., and Martinsen, J. (2006) Factors influencing mobile advertising acceptance: will incentives motivate college students to accept mobile advertisements? *International Journal of Mobile Marketing*, 1(1), 50–58.

Harris, P., Rettie, R., and Kwan, C. C. (2005) Adoption and Usage of m-commerce: a cross-cultural comparison of Hong Kong and the United Kingdom. *Journal of Electronic Commerce Research*, 6(3), 210–225.

Heinonen, K., and Strandvik, T. (2007) Consumer responsiveness to mobile marketing. *International Journal of Mobile Communications*, 5(6), 603–617.

Heller, N. E. (2006) Growth of mobile multimedia advertising. *International Journal of Mobile Marketing*, 1(1), 41–49.

Hosbond, J. H., and Skov, M. B. (2007) Micro mobility marketing: two cases on location-based supermarket shopping trolleys. *Journal of Targeting, Measurement and Analysis for Marketing*, 16(1), 68–78.

Hsu, H., Lu, H., and Hsu, C. (2008) Multimedia messaging service acceptance of pre- and post-adopters: a sociotechnical perspective. *International Journal of Mobile Communications*, 6(5), 598–615.

Jarvenpaa, S. L., Lang, K. R., Takeda, Y., and Tuunainen, V. K. (2003) Mobile commerce at crossroads. *Communications of the ACM*, 46(12), 41–44.

Junglas, I. A., Johnson, N. A., and Spitzmüller, C. (2008) Personality traits and concern for privacy: an empirical study in the context of location-based services. *European Journal of Information Systems*, 17(4), 387–403.

Karjaluoto, H., and Alatalo, T. (2007) Consumers' attitudes towards and intention to participate in mobile marketing.

International Journal of Services Technology and Management, 8(2/3), 155.

Karp, G. (2007) Mobile marketing and interactive promotions on mobile devices: navigating legal hurdles. *International Journal of Mobile Marketing*, 2(2), 78–85.

Khalifa, M., and Shen, K. N. (2008) Drivers for transactional B2C m-commerce adoption: extended theory of planned behavior. *The Journal of Computer Information Systems*, 48(3), 111–117.

Kim, B., and Han, I. (2009) What drives the adoption of mobile data services? An approach from a value perspective. *Journal of Information Technology*, 24, 35-45.

Kim, H., Lee, I., and Kim, J. (2008) Maintaining continuers vs. converting discontinuers: relative importance of post-adoption factors for mobile data services. *International Journal of Mobile Communications*, 6(1), 108–132.

Kleijnen, M., Ruyter, K., and Wetzels, M. (2004) Consumer adoption of wireless services: discovering the rules, while playing the game. *Journal of Interactive Marketing*, 18(2), 51–62.

Komulainen, H., Mainela, T., Tähtinen, J., and Ulkuniemi, P. (2007) Retailers' different value perceptions of mobile advertising service. *International Journal of Service Industry Management*, 18(4), 368–393.

Kondo, F. N., and Nakahara, M. (2007) Differences in customers' responsiveness to mobile direct mail coupon promotions. *International Journal of Mobile Marketing*, 2(2), 68–74.

Kumar, S., and Stokkeland, J. (2003) Evolution of GPS technology and its subsequent use in commercial markets.

International Journal of Mobile Communications, 1(1/2), 180–193.

Kumar, S., and Zahn, C. (2003) Mobile communications: evolution and impact on business operations. *Technovation*, 23(6), 515–521.

Laukkanen, T. (2005) Consumer value creation in mobile banking services. *International Journal of Mobile Communications*, 3(4), 325–338.

Lee, C., Cheng, H. K., and Cheng, H. (2007) An empirical study of mobile commerce in insurance industry: task-technology fit and individual differences. *Decision Support Systems*, 43(1), 95–110.

Lee, R., and Murphy, J. (2006) The consumption of mobile services by Australian university students. *International Journal of Mobile Marketing*, 1(1), 13–20.

Lee, T., and Jun, J. (2007) The role of contextual marketing offer in mobile commerce acceptance: comparison between mobile commerce users and nonusers. *International Journal of Mobile Communications*, 5(3), 339–356.

Lee, Y., Kim, J., Lee, I., and Kim, H. (2002) A cross-cultural study on the value structure of mobile Internet usage: comparison between Korea and Japan. *Journal of Electronic Commerce Research*, 3(4), 227–239.

Lembke, J. (2002) Mobile commerce and the creation of a marketplace. *The Journal of Policy, Regulation and Strategy for Telecommunications, Information and Media*, 4(3), 50–56.

Leppäniemi, M., Sinisalo, J., and Karjaluoto, H. (2006) A review of mobile marketing research. *International Journal of Mobile Marketing*, 1(1), 30–40.

Lin, H-H., and Wang, Y-S. (2006) An examination of the determinants of customer loyalty in mobile commerce contexts. *Information & Management*, 43(3), 271–282.

Lu, J., Yu, C., Liu, C., and Ku, C. Y. (2004) Wireless trust: conceptual and operational definition. *International Journal of Mobile Communications*, 2(1), 38–50.

Luarn, P., and Lin, H. (2005) Toward an understanding of the behavioral intention to use mobile banking, *Computers in Human Behavior*, 21, 873–891.

Maamar, Z. (2003) Commerce, e-commerce, and m-commerce: what comes next? *Communications of the ACM*, 46(12), 251–257.

MacInnes, I., Moneta, J., Caraballo, J., and Sarni, D. (2002) Business models for mobile content: the case of m-games. *Electronic Markets*, 12(4), 218–227.

Magura, B. (2003) What hooks m-commerce customers? *MIT Sloan Management Review*, 44(3), 9–16.

Malladi, R., and Agrawal, D. P. (2002) Current and future applications of mobile and wireless networks. *Communications of the ACM*, 45(10), 144–146.

Maneesoonthorn, C., and Fortin, D. (2006) Texting behavior and attitudes toward permission mobile advertising: an empirical study of mobile users' acceptance of SMS for marketing purposes. *International Journal of Mobile Marketing*, 1(1), 66–72.

Marez, L., Vyncke, P., Berte, K., Schuurman D., and Moor, K. (2007) Adopter segments, adoption determinants and mobile marketing. *Journal of Targeting, Measurement and Analysis for Marketing*, 16(1), 78–96.

Merisavo, M., Vesanen, J., Arponen, A., and Kajalo, S. (2006) The effectiveness of targeted mobile advertising in selling mobile services: an empirical study. *International Journal of Mobile Communications*, 4(2), 119–127.

Milne, G. R., and Rohm, A. J. (2003) The 411 on mobile privacy. *Marketing Management*, 12(4), 40–45.

Min, Q., and Ji, S. (2008) A meta-analysis of mobile commerce research in China (2002–2006) *International Journal of Mobile Communications*, 6(3). 390–403.

Nerger, P. (2008) Breaking free from "DOTCOM THINK-ING" in a mobile world. *International Journal of Mobile Marketing*, 3(1), 19N22.

Newell, J., and Meier, M. (2007) Desperately seeking opt-in: a field report from a student led mobile marketing initiative. *International Journal of Mobile Marketing*, 2(2), 53–57.

Ngai, E. W. T., and Gunasekaran, A. (2007) A review for mobile commerce research and applications. *Decision Support Systems*, 43, 3–15.

Nohria, N., and Leestma, M. (2001) A Moving Target: The Mobile-Commerce Customer. *MIT Sloan Management Review*, 42(3), 104–105.

Okazaki, S. (2004) How do Japanese consumers perceive wireless ads? A multivariate analysis. *International Journal of Advertising*, 23(4), 429–454.

Okazaki, S. (2005) Mobile advertising adoption by multinationals. *Internet Research*, 15(2), 160–180.

Okazaki, S. (2005) New perspectives on m-commerce research. *Journal of Electronic Commerce Research*, 6(3), 160–165.

Okazaki, S., Katsukura, A., and Nishiyama, M. (2007) How mobile advertising works: the role of trust in improving attitudes and recall. *Journal of Advertising Research*, 47(2), 165–178.

Okazaki, S., and Taylor, C. R. (2008) What is SMS advertising and why do multinationals adopt it? Answers from an empirical study in European markets. *Journal of Business Research*, 61(1), 4–12.

Oliva, R. A. (2003) Going mobile. *Marketing Management*, 12(4), 46–48.

Pagani, M. (2004) Determinants of adoption of third generation mobile multimedia services. *Journal of Interactive Marketing*, 18(3), 46.

Park, C. (2006) Hedonic and utilitarian values of mobile internet in Korea. *International Journal of Mobile Communications*, 4(5), 497–508.

Park, J., and SuJin Y. (2006) The moderating role of consumer trust and experiences: value driven usage of mobile technology. *International Journal of Mobile Marketing*, 1(2), 24–32.

Pedersen, P. E. (2005) Adoption of mobile Internet services: an exploratory study of mobile commerce early adopters. *Journal of Organizational Computing and Electronic Commerce*, 15 (2), 203–222.

Petty, R. D. (2003) Wireless advertising messaging: Legal analysis and public policy issues. *Journal of Public Policy & Marketing*, 22(1), 71–82.

Pihlström, M. (2007) Committed to content provider or mobile channel? Determinants of continuous mobile multimedia service use. *JITTA: Journal of Information Technology Theory and Application*, 9(1), 1–24.

Pura, M. (2005) Linking perceived value and loyalty in location-based mobile services. *Managing Service Quality,* 15(6), 509–539.

Ramkumar, G. D. (2007) Image recognition as a method for opt-in and applications for mobile marketing. *International Journal of Mobile Marketing,* 2(2), 42–49.

Rao, B., and Minakakis, L. (2003) Evolution of mobile location-based services. *Communications of the ACM,* 46(12), 61–65.

Ratten, V. (2008) Technological innovations in the m-commerce industry: a conceptual model of WAP banking intentions. *Journal of High Technology Management Research,* 18, 111–117.

Reid, F. J. M., and Reid, D. J. (2010) The expressive and conversational affordances of mobile messaging. *Behaviour & Information Technology,* 29(1), 3–22.

Rohm, A. J., and Sultan, F. (2006) An exploratory cross-market study of mobile marketing acceptance. *International Journal of Mobile Marketing,* 1(1), 4–12.

Scornavacca, E., Barnes, S. J., and Huff, S. L. (2006) mobile business research published in 2000–2004: emergence, current status and future opportunities. *Communications of AIS,* 17, 2–19.

Scornavacca, E., and McKenzie, J. (2007) Unveiling managers' perceptions of the critical success factors for SMS based campaigns. *International Journal of Mobile Communications,* 5(4), 445–456.

Senn, J. A. (2000) The emergence of m-commerce. *Computer,* 33(12), 148–151.

Shugan, S. M. (2004) The impact of advancing technology on marketing and academic research. *Marketing Science,* 23(4), 469–476.

Siau, K., Lim, E., and Shen, Z. (2001) Mobile commerce: Promises, challenges, and research agenda. *Journal of Database Management*, 12(3), 4–14.

Stafford, T. F., and Gillenson, M. L. (2003) Mobile commerce: what it is and what it could be? *Communications of the ACM*, 46(12), 33–34.

Steinbock, D. (2006) The missing link: why mobile marketing is different? *International Journal of Mobile Marketing*, 1(1), 83–94.

Sultan, F., and Rohm, A. (2005) The coming era of "brand in the hand" marketing. *MIT Sloan Management Review*, 47(1), 83–90.

Sultan, F., and Rohm, A. J. (2008) How to market to generation m(obile). *MIT Sloan Management Review*, 49(4), 35–41.

Sundqvist, S., Frank, L., and Puumalainen, K. (2005) The effects of country characteristics, cultural similarity and adoption timing on the diffusion of wireless communications. *Journal of Business Research*, 58(1), 107–110.

Swilley, E., and Hofacker, C. F. (2006) Defining mobile commerce in a marketing context. *International Journal of Mobile Marketing*, 1(2), 18–23.

Tsang, M. M., Ho, S., and Liang, T. (2004) Consumer attitudes toward mobile advertising: an empirical study. *International Journal of Electronic Commerce*, 8(3), 65–78.

Varnali, K., and Toker, A. (2010) Mobile marketing research: the-state-of-the-art. *International Journal of Information Management*, 30, 144–151.

Varnali, K., and Yilmaz, C. (2010) Exploring the Mobile Consumer. In I. Lee (ed.), *Encyclopedia of E-Business Develop-*

ment and Management in the Global Economy. Hershey, PA: IGI-Global, pp. 768–778.

Varshney, U. (2005) Vehicular mobile commerce: applications, challenges, and research problems. *Communications of the Association for Information Systems*, 16, 329–339.

Varshney, U., and Vetter, R. (2002) Mobile commerce: framework, applications and networking support. *Mobile Networks and Applications*, 7(3), 185–199.

Vatanparast, R., and Asil, M. (2007) Factors affecting the use of mobile advertising. *International Journal of Mobile Marketing*, 2(2), 21–34.

Wang, A. (2007) Branding over mobile and Internet advertising: the cross-media effect. *International Journal of Mobile Marketing*, 2(1), 34–42.

Wang, Y., Lin, H., and Luarn, P. (2006) Predicting consumer intention to use mobile service. *Information Systems Journal*, 16(2), 157.

Wareham, J. D., Busquets, X., and Austin, R. D. (2009) Creative, convergent, and social: prospects for mobile computing. *Journal of Information Technology*, 24, 139–143.

Watson, R. T., Pitt, L. F., Berthon, P., and Zinkhan, G. M. (2002) U-commerce: expanding the universe of marketing. *Academy of Marketing Science Journal*, 30(4), 333–348.

Weitenberner, C., Chapman, M., Miranda, G., Tobar, S., Wagoner, E., and Akasaki, D. (2006) United States and south east Asian mobile markets: a comparative analysis of infrastructure and cultural differences. *International Journal of Mobile Marketing*, 1(1), 73–82.

Wen, H. J., and Mahatanankoon, P. (2004) M-commerce operation modes and applications. *International Journal of Electronic Business*, 2(3), 301.

Worthy, J., and Graham, N. (2002) Electronic marketing: new rules for electronic marketing—an obstacle to m-commerce? *Computer Law & Security Report*, 18(2), 106–109.

Wu, J. H., and Hisa, T. L. (2008) Developing e-business dynamic capabilities: an analysis of e-commerce innovation from i-, m-, to u-commerce. *Journal of Organizational Computing and Electronic Commerce*, 18, 95–111.

Xu, D. J. (2006/2007) The influence of personalization in affecting consumer attitudes toward mobile advertising in China. *The Journal of Computer Information Systems*, 47(2), 9–20.

Yang, K., and Jolly, L. D. (2006) Value-added mobile data services: the antecedent effects of consumer value on using mobile data services. *International Journal of Mobile Marketing*, 1(2), 11–17.

Yang, K. C. C. (2005) Exploring factors affecting the adoption of mobile commerce in Singapore. *Telematics & Informatics*, 22(3), 257–277.

Zeng, E. Y., Yen, D. C., Hwang, H., and Huang, S. (2003) Mobile commerce: the convergence of e-commerce and wireless technology. *International Journal of Services Technology and Management*, 4(3), 302.

Related Web Sites

Center for Digital Democracy: http://www.democraticmedia.org
CDD, a not-for-profit group based in Washington, D.C., works to promote an electronic media system that fosters democratic expression and human rights. It keeps track of the commercial media market. Through its monitoring and analysis of new media marketplace developments, CDD has served as an early warning system for journalists, policymakers, and the public about emerging public interest issues.

Direct Marketing Association: http://www.the-dma.org
The DMA is the leading global trade association of businesses and nonprofit organizations using and supporting multichannel direct marketing tools and techniques. DMA advocates industry standards for responsible marketing and promotes research, education, and networking opportunities to improve results throughout the end-to-end direct marketing process.

European Telecommunications Standards Institute: http://www.etsi.org
The European Telecommunications Standards Institute (ETSI) produces globally-applicable standards for information and

communications technologies (ICT), including fixed, mobile, radio, converged, broadcast, and Internet technologies.

GOMO News: http://www.gomonews.com

GoMo News provides news about the mobile ecosystem on a daily basis. It is a social media site for the B2B mobile industry.

GSM Association: http://www.gsmworld.com

The GSMA represents the interests of the worldwide mobile communications industry. Spanning 219 countries, the GSMA unites nearly 800 of the world's mobile operators, as well as more than 200 companies in the broader mobile ecosystem, including handset makers, software companies, equipment providers, Internet companies, and media and entertainment organizations.

International Telecommunication Union: http://www.itu.int

The ITU is the leading United Nations agency for information and communication technology issues, and the global focal point for governments and the private sector in developing networks and services. The ITU coordinates the shared global use of the radio spectrum, promotes international cooperation in assigning satellite orbits, works to improve telecommunication infrastructure in the developing world, and establishes the worldwide standards that foster seamless interconnection of a vast range of communications systems.

Mobile Consumer Lab at the International University of Japan: http://mocobe.com

The Web site of the Mobile Consumer Lab at the International University of Japan provides resources on a number of topics related to the impact of mobile and wireless technologies on consumer behavior.

Mobile Entertainment Forum: http://www.m-e-f.org

MEF, founded in 2000, is a global trade association for companies large and small across the mobile entertainment value chain. It actively promotes the mobile entertainment industry as an identifiable and significant sector, with specific commercial structures and interests, and it creates a focal point for the industry to work together on global issues and local priorities to accelerate the industry's growth.

Mobile Marketer: http://www.mobilemarketer.com

Mobile Marketer is a news publication that was launched in 2007. It offers news and analysis on mobile marketing, media, and commerce.

Mobile Marketing Association: http://www.mmaglobal.com

The MMA is the premier global association that strives to stimulate the growth of mobile marketing and its associated technology. MMA members include agencies, advertisers, handheld device manufacturers, carriers and operators, retailers, software providers, and service providers, as well as any company focused on the potential of marketing via mobile devices.

Mobile Marketing Magazine: http://www.mobilemarketingmagazine.co.uk/

This is a regularly updated online magazine dedicated to mobile marketing.

Mobile Web Best Practices: http://www.w3.org/TR/mobile-bp

This document specifies best practices for delivering Web content to mobile devices. It is primarily directed at creators, maintainers, and operators of Web sites.

Mobile Monday Global: http://www.mobilemonday.net
Mobile Monday is a global community of mobile industry visionaries, developers, and influencers fostering cooperation and cross-border business development through virtual and live networking events for the purpose of sharing ideas, best practices, and trends from global markets.

Open Mobile Alliance: http://www.wapforum.com
OMA is an industry forum formed in June 2002 by nearly 200 companies to facilitate global user adoption of mobile data services by specifying market-driven mobile service enablers that ensure service interoperability across devices, geographies, service providers, operators, and networks while allowing businesses to compete through innovation and differentiation.

Sociology of the Mobile Phone: http://www.socio.ch/mobile
This is an academic Web site edited by Prof. Hans Gesser, professor of sociology at Universität Zürich. It publishes online articles focusing on the social impact of mobile phones.

Telecommunications Industry Association: http://www.tiaonline.org
TIA is a trade association representing its 600 members through standards development, government affairs, business opportunities, market intelligence, certification, and worldwide environmental regulatory compliance. Since its foundation, it has advocated numerous policy issues for the benefit of its members and sponsored engineering committees that set standards determining the pace of development in the industry.

Wi-Fi Planet: http://www.wi-fiplanet.com
This site contains daily news, features, reviews, and tutorials covering a wide range of issues regarding the wireless LAN universe.

Wireless Week: http://www.wirelessweek.com
This Web site is regularly updated and releases news, opinions, analyses, and forums about the wireless world.

Wireless World Research Forum: http://www.wireless-world-research.org
The Forum is a global organization founded in August 2001. It represents all sectors of the mobile communications industry and the research community. The objective of the forum is to formulate ideas on strategic future research directions in the wireless field, among industry and academia, and to generate, identify, and promote research areas and technical trends for mobile and wireless system technologies.

Glossary*

Acquisition Rate   Percentage of respondents who opted in to participate in a mobile marketing initiative.

Ad Impression   Total number of advertisement exposures.

Advergaming   Embedding marketing messages within mobile games or the use of mobile games with marketing-related purposes.

Affiliate Marketing   Affiliate marketing is a revenue-sharing–oriented business model in which one mobile Web site creates traffic to another Web site in return for monetary benefits.

Aggregator   Company that stands between content providers and network operators to provide several key value-added services such as business simplification, digital rights management, and settling payment issues between its clients.

*Adapted from Mobile Marketing Association's Industry Glossary http://mmaglobal .com/glossary.pdf

Airtime	Total number of connected minutes consumed by a mobile subscriber for engaging in a particular mobile service.
Application	Software solution that provides the necessary platform for implementing the business logic of a particular mobile marketing initiative.
Asynchronous	A type of two-way communication that occurs with a time delay, allowing participants to respond at their own convenience.
Average Revenue per User (ARPU)	Average revenue generated by a user.
Bandwidth	Rate of data transmission, measured in bits per second (bps), kilobits per second (kbps), or megabits per second (mbps).
Bluetooth	A communication protocol that enables devices to send and receive data wirelessly over short ranges, using the 2.4 GHz spectrum band.
Call to Action	A statement or instruction embedded in advertising messages that encourages opt-in and explains how to respond to a particular marketing initiative.
Carrier	See mobile network operator

Cell Broadcast   A technology that allows a text or binary message to be distributed to all mobile terminals connected to a set of cells or towers in a specified area.

Click-Through Rate   The ratio of mobile users who clicked on an ad on a mobile Web site to the total number of times the ad was seen by Web site visitors.

Click to Call   A service that enables a mobile user to initiate a voice call to a prespecified phone number by clicking on a link or a banner on a mobile Web site.

Content Provider   Company that develops digital rich media content for the mobile medium.

Cookie   A parcel of information sent by a server to a Web browser and then sent back unchanged by the browser each time it accesses that server. HTTP cookies are used for authenticating, tracking, and maintaining specific information about users.

Cost per Acquisition (CPA)   Pricing based on customer acquisition on behalf of the advertiser brand or on the elicited customer response.

Cost per Click (CPC)   Pricing based on actual click-throughs.

Cost per Listen (CPL)	Pricing based on the actual number of users who listened to an advertisement for more than a specified duration (e.g., five seconds).
Cost per Thousand Impressions (CPM)	A metric used to price mobile banners.
Data Charging	The cost of using mobile data services such as using mobile Internet or downloading mobile content.
Digital Multimedia Broadcasting	A digital transmission technology for sending multimedia to mobile handsets.
Digital Video Broadcasting-Handset (Dvb-H)	A digital transmission technology used for mobile TV that combines the traditional digital video and the IP that scales for smaller devices.
Double Opt-In	The process of confirming a subscriber's opt-in with a second confirmation request.
Dual Band	A mobile device that supports and is compatible with two different bands or frequencies.
Enhanced Data Rates for GSM Evolution (Edge) and 3G	An intermediate technology between 2G that enables data speeds of up to 384 kbps.

Enhanced Message Service (EMS)	An application level extension to SMS that enables short text messages to include special text formatting and predefined simple graphics.
General Packet Radio Service (GPRS)	A packet switching technology that enables high-speed data transmission of up to 115 kbps.
Global Positioning System (GPS)	A technology that enables triangulation of one's location on Earth by using time differences between signals from various satellites to reach the receiving device.
Global System for Mobile Communications (GSM)	A digital mobile cellular standard developed to provide the underlying infrastructure of mobile communications. It is the main 2G digital wireless standard.
I-Mode	A packet-based information service developed by Japanese operator DoCoMo to deliver a wide range of services to its subscribers.
Impressions	A metric used to count the number of times an advertisement is seen by mobile users.
Interactive Voice Response (IVR)	A system that allows users to interact with an automated communications system over the phone. An IVR system prompts users with a prerecorded script and then requires a response from the user either orally or by pressing a touchtone key.

International Mobile Equipment Identity (IMEI)	A 15-digit, unique number assigned to each mobile phone. The serial number represents the manufacturer, model, assembly code, and serial number of the mobile device.
Interstitial Ad	An advertising message that is inserted into the middle of a complete MMS message.
Java	An object-oriented programming language developed by Sun Microsystems, which does not rely on any operating system to work as long as the Java Virtual Machine is installed.
Landing Page	A Web page to which users are directed when they click on a mobile ad banner or a link.
Location-Based Services (Lbss)	A range of services provided to mobile subscribers resulting from the knowledge of their geographical location.
Mobile Coupon	An electronic ticket delivered to mobile handsets that can be exchanged for a financial discount or rebate when a product or service is purchased.
Mobile Marketing Association (Mma)	A global nonprofit organization established to lead the growth of mobile marketing and its associated technologies and to set up industry regulations and best practices for the use of the mobile channel for marketing purposes.

Mobile Network Operator	Telecommunication company that provides the infrastructure for mobile communications, including transportation, transmission, and switching for voice and data.
Mobile Search	A search through the mobile Internet.
Mobile Subscriber	An individual who signs an agreement with a mobile operator in order to use wireless telecommunication services.
Mobile Virtual Network Operator (MVNO)	A company that does not own a licensed frequency spectrum like a traditional carrier but rather resells services under its own brand name using the network of another mobile operator.
Monotone	A ringtone that plays one musical note at a time.
Multimedia Messaging Service (MMS)	A messaging standard that can incorporate pictures, audio, and video clips.
Opt-In	The process by which users give explicit consent to receive specific advertising messages on their mobile devices.
Opt-Out	The process by which users cancel their prior consent to receive specific advertising messages on their mobile devices.

Page View — A metric that measures the number of times a mobile Web page is viewed by users.

Polyphonic Ringtone — Audio ringtone created with MIDI technology to be used on mobile handsets.

Premium Rate — Charges that are above the standard text messaging charges applied by the mobile operator.

Prepaid — No-contract mobile subscription in which the user purchases credits in advance for the use of a mobile network operators wireless telecommunication services.

Pull Messaging — Content is sent to users' mobile devices upon their explicit request, on a one-time basis.

Push Messaging — Content is sent to users' mobile devices without their explicit request.

Referring Page — The mobile Web page that directs the visitor to the landing page.

Relevance — The extent to which a message is interesting or useful to target users.

Ringback Tone (RBT) — The audible ringing sound that is heard on the telephone line by the calling party after dialing and prior to the call being answered at the receiving end. Can be replaced by a musical tone or a voice clip.

Roaming	A service that allows mobile subscribers to be able to use their mobile devices on the networks of operators other than their contracted one.
Short Message Service (SMS)	A messaging standard that allows 160 character text-only format.
Synchronous	A type of two-way communication that allows participants to respond in real time, with no time delay.
Targeting	The process of selecting consumer segments that have homogeneous customer profiles for marketing communication in order to establish criteria for personalization of the marketing message and to increase the effectiveness of the marketing campaign.
3G	The abbreviation for the third generation of wireless service, which is characterized by high data speeds, always-on data access, and greater voice capacity. Data transmission rates range from 144 kbps to more than 2 mbps.
Transcoding	The optimization of multimedia ads to make them appear and sound best on different mobile devices based on device capabilities.

Value-Added Service (VAS)	Mobile services that add value to the standard services provided by mobile operators.
Wireless Application Protocol (WAP)	The predominant international communication protocol used to bring Internet-based content and value-added services to mobile devices.
WAP Push	A WAP link that is inserted into an SMS message that allows delivery of WAP content to users' mobile devices with minimum user effort.

Index

About the Authors

Kaan Varnali, Ph.D., has been conducting research on mobile marketing for more than three years at Bogazici University, Turkey. His research has appeared in several scholarly outlets as journal articles and book chapters. He has a particular interest in mobile consumer behavior, especially on the factors that drive consumers' value creation process through mobile experiences. His other research areas include various topics related to marketing through social media. He is currently an assistant professor at Istanbul Bilgi University, Turkey, where he teaches courses on new media and consumer behavior.

Aysegul Toker, Ph.D., is a professor and the chair at the Department of Management, Bogazici University, Turkey, where she teaches courses on management information systems, e-business models, customer relationship management, database marketing, and data-mining applications. She has articles published in the areas of digital marketing, online communities, mobile applications, business excellence, total quality management, decision support systems, and production management. Her current research interests include mobile marketing, e-business/e-commerce, customer relationship management, customer-knowledge management, and customer-focused strategies.

Cengiz Yılmaz, Ph.D., is a professor of marketing at Bogazici University, Turkey. He obtained his Ph.D. in marketing from Texas Tech University in 1999. His research interests focus on distribution channels and relationship marketing, emerging technologies and their impacts on marketing applications, and strategic issues concerning intra- and interfirm aspects in marketing systems and their links with business performance. His research has been published in several scholarly journals including *Journal of the Academy of Marketing Science, European Journal of Marketing, Journal of Business Research, Industrial Marketing Management, Journal of World Business, International Small Business Journal,* and *Journal of Business and Industrial Marketing.*